TRANSITIONAL MINISTRY

A TIME OF OPPORTUNITY

MOLLY DALE SMITH, EDITOR

with a foreword by

LOREN MEAD

Church Publishing
NEW YORK

Library of Congress Cataloging-in-Publication Data

Transitional ministry : a time of opportunity / Molly Dale Smith, editor ; with a foreword by Loren Mead.

p. cm.

Includes bibliographical references.

ISBN 978-0-89869-622-6 (pbk.)

1. Interim clergy. 2. Change--Religious aspects--Christianity. I. Smith, Molly Dale. II. Title.

BV676.3.T73 2009

253--dc22

2009010198

Church Publishing, Incorporated.
445 Fifth Avenue
New York, New York 10016

www.churchpublishing.com

5   4   3   2   1

Contents

FOREWORD

HOW DID IT ALL GET STARTED?

LOREN MEAD

For many of us in the churches, the idea of an "interim pastor" comes as a new idea. We hear the word "interim" or "transition" applied to ministry and we wonder, is this the new kid on the block? In one way it is—the first actual conference to unpack the idea of the interim pastorate occurred in 1975—just yesterday when you realize that the churches went some 1,930 years or so without such a role for some of its pastors.

There are two other reasons it's not well known. First, few if any "ordinary" ordained clergy have ever experienced being in a congregation that's going through an "interim." And the laity who make up the membership of congregations have tended to think of such periods as "awkward" and "uncomfortable," a time when they experience a lot of things being unglued in their congregation and a lot of uncertainty. Most clergy, in fact, don't know beans about what interim ministry is all about. They've never been through one. All too many of them have a subconscious desire to extend their pastorates—trying to engineer the appointment of an associate or someone else who thinks as they do to become the interim pastor. I call that "trying to rule from beyond the grave." It rarely works well for the congregation.

Bishops and executives, on the other hand, tend to see what we now call "interims" as taking up a lot of their time in a way that has come to feel like a crap-shoot—sometimes you roll a 7 or 11, but more often you end up crapping out. Ignoring real signs of a need for rethinking ministry and leadership needs, they get steam rollered by the anxiety of the congregation to "Hurry up! We need a new pastor now!" or the belief that "that place will go to hell in a hand-basket if I don't get somebody in there right away!"

iv

I need to point out that all we've learned about the interim time gives the lie to such worrisome thoughts. Most congregations do have some anxious times during an interim. But when their bishops and their own better selves overcome their anxiety, the period of the interim is almost always experienced as a time of growth of lay leadership as well as of clarity about their identity and mission.

The second reason for misconceptions about this ministry is that our understanding of ministry itself has undergone a sea change in the past few decades. What we now call an "interim" we used to call a "vacancy." That change of language covers a vast change in what we understand by "ministry." Our old language expressed our belief that there was no ministry present if there were no ordained pastor. So we called this the period of "vacancy." That understanding of ministry is still with us much of the time. Today we label this way of thinking "clericalism." It is long outdated, but it is deeply ingrained in many of us. We still think, at some instinctual level, that the presence of clergy means that ministry is happening and where there are no clergy, there really isn't any ministry going on. Using the term "interim" instead of "vacancy" makes the point that ministry belongs to the people of the congregation." Clergy people come and go, but the ministry is already there.

Most called clergy assume, from that outdated concept of ministry that they pick up along the way, that when they come to the parish, they bring ministry on their backs—that the ministry is theirs to define, establish, and implement.

Interim pastors are trained to know that's poppycock. Ministry is already there when they get there. It has been there and it will still be there when they leave. For a short time they have the privilege of bringing their skills and insights to the ministry that's there on the ground already. And they use their skills to free up and strengthen the ministry they find; in some cases clearing out noxious underbrush that's grown up around the edges, in some cases helping people get over the losses they've experienced—not least the loss of their previous pastor. In other cases, they are helping the parish reconnect to its denominational family; in still other cases, nurturing those who are discerning new roles in the life of the congregation, and always, in every interim, working to discover the new call to ministry that's challenging them to mission.

The first person I know of who undertook to be an interim pastor was a Presbyterian pastor, Keith Irwin, whose story I told in my first book, *New Hope For Congregations* (Seabury, 1972). At the time—between 1969 and 1973, before the Alban Institute was born—I was working in an Episcopal Church action-research program that we called "Project Test Pattern." After a few abortive efforts, we began experimenting with the use of a skill beginning to be in use in management circles in universities, corporations, and government—what we called "organizational development." We began testing the use of "OD" consultants, as we called them, as change agents to help local congregations be more effective and faithful in their work.

As we prepared to train a new batch of such consultants, Keith came to me with the suggestion that he be trained as a consultant, and then use those skills as a "supply pastor" in a congregation that had had a troubled past, and whose pastor had been terminated under a cloud. I said "Yes," because I was focused on using the skills of change in a congregation. He got the training, did his work in South Dakota, and I worked as his long-distance supervisor. I even went to visit the congregation after he left to try to understand the impact of his work there. In the back of my mind I realized his work was different from the other consultants, because he was working where the "permanent pastor" was gone, working where there had been some obvious trauma between pastor and congregation.

I wrote his story simply as a story of an attempt to change a congregation and a story of how consulting skills could be used in congregations. The penny was in the process of beginning to drop for me that I was dealing with something new with transition in pastoral leadership. In the next year or so, our action-research at "Project Test Pattern" did further study of that critical point of transition of leadership (still misidentified as "The Vacancy Consultation Project"—you can see that the penny had not fully dropped yet).

After the Episcopal Project Test Pattern closed at the end of 1973, one of the first things I focused on in our newly founded ecumenical Alban Institute was that issue of transition. We worked first at how new pastors "started up" in new positions. (That research eventually led to "Fresh Start.") And, nearly two years after Keith Irwin brought the subject up, a retired Episcopal priest, Felix Kloman, pushed me further. He encouraged me to try to mobilize some of the first-class clergy who were entering retirement. He and I saw a particularly talented and skilled resource being underutilized by the church at the same time that we had dozens of congregations facing pastoral change. Many of those congregations really needed some pastoral care and even therapy during the transitions. Keith Irwin, bringing new skills, had begun defining a new way to go beyond "hand holding" of anxious congregations, to skilled intervention at the point of transition.

That time, the penny did drop. I managed to put together an exploratory conference of experienced pastors who were already working on "interims," "vacancy ministries," "locum tenens" placements, and "supply ministries." Keith Irwin was one those whom we invited to the meeting. The common element was that they saw this transition moment not as a problem, but as a moment of extraordinary potential—potential both for sorting out and cleaning up problems from the past, and also clearing the way for a new pastoral appointment.

We gathered a lot of new information out of the St. Louis conference and—because about ten denominational executives also attended—we began to broaden the base of interest in interim pastorates. A training program for interim pastors and interim consultants was then designed by the Mid Atlantic Training Committee, an ecumenical training network led by John Denham of Washington, DC, and various denominations began adapting the model to their work.

Our next initiative came as we realized how isolated these interim pastors were—facing the difficulty of finding places and jobs into which to relocate every year or eighteen months, generally not being understood by other clergy or even—often—by the judicatory systems that could deploy them. We saw that this group of clergy really had no advocates within their denominational systems, nor did they have support systems such as those already in place for more permanently placed clergy. So, with a small foundation grant and with the leadership of Roy Oswald, we spent several years assisting at the birth of what has now become the Interim Ministry Network (IMN), an ecumenical, self-supporting, national network now nearly three decades years old.

From the beginnings in St. Louis, the work was understood to be very denominational; the placement processes were integral to each denomination's ways of doing things. But at the same time what we were doing was radically interdenominational. The critical interactions by which pastors move from one position to another are ruled by denominational canons or laws—but the dynamics of what happens, the emotions of the people involved, and the processes of leadership in each transition were deeply congruent with each other. The issues were totally interdenominational, but each congregation and each pastor dealt with them within their own denominational structures. Several denominations formed what we think of as "fellowship groups" of interim pastors of that denomination—to interpret the work there; to educate clergy, laity, and executives; and to lobby, where needed, for better system support. The Presbyterian group was strengthened by the presence of Allen Gripe; the Episcopalians by Rip Coffin, Philip Porcher, and Charles Vache—himself a bishop. Many such denominational groups continue to meet at the annual meeting of the IMN.

The IMN now manages regular training programs for those who want to become interim pastors. It maintains communication with and occasional training for denominational executives. It publishes information in a journal; it has annual conferences for its 1,000 members; and it continues the conversation and research about this model of ministry and supports and educates about its set of standards. Equally important, it attempts to advocate for healthy processes in judicatories for managing pastoral transitions.

There is unfinished business for the network and for those in interim pastorates in the task of educating religious systems to the style of leadership that it has both discovered and exemplifies—a style that sees the ordained clergy person not as *the* ministry, but as the *servant of* the ministry. That clarity demands a new role for the clergy—not as "possessors" of ministry, but as enhancers, strengtheners, and sometimes even janitors of ministry. The interim pastor stands for a model of leadership for all the clergy of the church.

The new kid on the block has come of age. The interim pastorate is no longer an unknown at the fringes of the life of the churches. It is established in three particulars:

1. Hundreds of interim pastors are at work today, strengthening our churches in a special, "in-between the times" kind of pastorate. That work goes on.

2. The whole concept of the ordained pastorate is being challenged by a very old but rediscovered truth long hidden behind a clerical model of the church: the reality of a ministry of a church of the laity.

3. The conviction, acted on by interim pastors and by hundreds of faithful laity, clergy, bishops, and denominational executives, that points of leadership transition are critical moments of opportunity for new hope for congregations.

This book builds on these simple realities. Ministry is already there when you get there. And it will be there when you leave. For a short time (or even a longer time, for the "settled" pastor) one has the extraordinary opportunity and privilege of collaborating with the ministers of God in that place, bringing your own gifts to that ministry. Then moving on, leaving—hopefully—stronger ministry because of having been there.

Acknowledgments

A special word of thanks goes to all of our colleagues in transitional ministry. As David A. Donges, bishop in the Evangelical Lutheran Church in America, has said, they are the "unsung heroes of the church."[1] Because these women and men have accepted the call to serve as intentional interim pastors and consultants, many in the church have learned the value of this ministry. The goal of this book is to widen the circle of those who appreciate transitional ministry.

Each author has changed details in order to protect the privacy of both individuals and congregations. Some readers may believe they can identify persons or locations because of the similarity to situations or persons they know. However, the stories in Section I of this book are not isolated, one-time-only events; rather, they are examples of things that occur in many places and in many denominations. The stories in Section II, while located in specific times and places, are illustrative of possibilities in other times and places. While we have tried hard to be accurate and faithful in the telling of our stories, we do accept responsibility for any errors that we may have made.

On behalf of all the authors in this book, I want to acknowledge the important contributions of our families and friends as well as the churches that we have served.

I especially want to express my gratitude to the members of Transitional Ministries in the Episcopal Church (TMEC). Their wisdom and support has been invaluable during the writing of this book. The current understanding of transitional ministry is founded on the labors of the pioneers of this movement. We cannot overestimate the contributions of our departed friend and colleague, the Rev. Rip Coffin, a founder of the Interim Ministry Network.

Editor Susie Erdey understood the vision for this book from the beginning and has been a continuing source of encouragement—thank you, Susie! Finally, my continuing thanks go to my husband, Richard, who supports me in every way.

Molly Dale Smith
Ash Wednesday 2009

1. http://www.elca.org/Growing-In-Faith/Ministry/Interim-Ministry-Association/Resources/Bishop-Donges.aspx

SECTION I

QUESTIONS ABOUT
TRANSITIONAL MINISTRY

Chapter 1

WHAT IS TRANSITIONAL MINISTRY?

MOLLY DALE SMITH

From the earliest days of my experience in transitional ministry, there have always been those who have asked, "Don't you want to be a real priest?" This hurtful question, not easy to hear, was always asked by good, well-meaning people—often the very people who really seemed to respond to my ministry. They thought they were taking my side and encouraging me to advance in my professional life. The truth is that transitional ministry is real ministry that meets real needs. As I moved from place to place, I always discovered the same lack of understanding of this ministry. This book is an attempt to clear up misunderstanding and to answer questions about transitional ministry. If you have ever encountered a major change in the life of your congregation, this is for you. And if you or your congregation have never experienced change, it is only a matter of time. As Bob Dylan reminds us, times are a-changin'.[1]

Recently I had to fill out a form that required me to list my addresses for the past ten years. I knew I had moved frequently but had never counted the number of moves. I was surprised to discover that I had lived at eight different places in those ten years. No wonder attending to change and its consequences is important to me! But the fact is that even those who have lived in the same house, driven the same streets, and gone to the same church for years are impacted by change. It creeps into every nook and cranny of twenty-first century life. With cell phones and the Internet, indispensable to daily life for most of us, we discover that we don't have to move to encounter a new environment. While change has always has been part of life, the fast pace of life today makes attending to change unavoidable. And the church is no different from any other aspect of life. Many wish their church to be a stable harbor in a sea of change, but this is not the reality. The question is not *will* we encounter change, but *how* will we respond?

1

What do we mean when we use this word "change"? *The Stanford Dictionary of Philosophy* begins an article on the subject with this caution: "Change is so pervasive in our lives that it almost defeats description and analysis." Nevertheless, any church member can tell you exactly what change is: Something is different. The pastor is called to a new position; the resulting feelings of helplessness heighten anxiety. Rapid growth is another kind of change. Our familiar church is filled with strange faces and we cannot find a place to park. The comfortable haven of memory has become a place of strange and often unsettling ways.

A change may impact not just the local congregation but the entire community. When Hurricane Katrina wreaked havoc on the Gulf Coast, Americans wanted to do something, to make it better in some way. We sent cases of water and boxes of food. A similar response followed 9/11. These horrific changes struck a deep chord in our hearts. We did what we could to help. My daughter, Andrea, was living in Manhattan on 9/11. I wanted to take away the pain of the disaster, but I couldn't. Andrea and her New York friends had to learn together what this catastrophe meant to them. During the days following, there were decisions to make about the safety of life in the city. Some of her friends left; she quit her job and moved closer to downtown to start a business.

About fifteen years ago, I went to a seminar about grief hosted by a local funeral home. The speaker made the point that any change results in grief. This concept intrigued me. Change, a difference in circumstance, whether good, bad, or indifferent, always results in some grief. The example given in the seminar came from an episode of the old TV show *All in the Family*. Archie Bunker had been given a promotion at work but the promotion meant that he could no longer be a member of his bowling team. The promotion was great—more money, more status—but Archie lost his place in the community.

In spite of many challenges to this hypothesis, I have yet to find an example of a change which did not result in some kind of loss and, hence, ensuing grief. This may seem to be a strong statement; however, a quick review of the grief cycle described by Elizabeth Kübler-Ross can help us to understand the varied responses elicited by change. In this theory, grief can be shown in the following behaviors: shock, denial, anger, bargaining, depression, testing, and acceptance. While Kübler-Ross's work is best known for its application to death and dying, Wikipedia points out that

> Kübler-Ross originally applied these stages to any form of catastrophic personal loss. Others have noticed that any significant personal change can elicit these changes. . . . Additionally the change in circumstances does not always have to be a negative one, just significant enough to cause a grief response to the loss (Scire, 2007). Accepting a new work position, for example, causes one to lose their routine, workplace friendships, familiar drive to work, or even customary lunch sources.[2]

The reality is that change has varied and often unexpected impacts on both individuals and groups.

William Bridges, in *Managing Transitions*, describes change as situational (new minister, new building) and external. Because change is external, we often have no control over it. The real source of our anxiety is transition, "the psychological process people go through to come to terms with the new situation."[3] Because Bridges' definitions provide the framework upon which this book rests, further elucidation of his thinking is worthwhile.

> The starting point for transition is not the outcome *but the ending you will have to make to leave the old situation behind.* Situational change hinges on the new thing, but psychological transition depends on letting go of the old reality and the old identity you had before the change took place. Nothing so undermines organizational change as the failure to think through who will have to let go of what when change occurs.[4]

I am reminded of the familiar saying, "Those who fail to plan, plan to fail." Lack of meaningful attention to transition is failure to plan.

Transitional ministry refers to the ministry that takes place during the time of transition. The transitional minister leads the congregation through the various processes needed to work on issues arising out of the change. At the same time, this clergy person is also responsible for the ongoing ministry and responsibilities typical of the settled pastor.

The helplessness experienced during change can be replaced by exercising responsibility. Obstacles presented by change can be turned into opportunity during transition. This premise is the key to transitional ministry and to this book. Change will always be part of life, as will the period of transition that is the result. Each change and its accompanying transition confront us with an opportunity. We can allow ourselves to be overwhelmed by feelings of anxiety, loss, anger, and even desperation, or we can embrace this opportunity to create a better future.

In my experience, congregations often are unprepared to deal with transition. People assume that life can go on as in the past, so the new feelings brought about by change are ignored. Each of the contributors to this book agrees that life is different—not necessarily worse—but different following major change. We, the writers, want to share with you the tools we have gained through our training and experience.

The overarching image for this book is kitchen-table conversation. Imagine that you have told me about some major change in your congregation. You have many questions and much uncertainty about how to move forward. So, I have invited you to my house. Others who are transition experts have joined us. We sit around my kitchen table drinking coffee. You ask questions: "What do we do first? What about conflict—already people are taking sides. Will change continue? How do we make plans now? Can't we keep it positive?" In turn, each person addresses your concerns. When all have spoken, you may feel calm. You may have a sense of the issues and opportunities that lie ahead. This book is that kitchen-table conversation. It is our hope that reading this book will prepare you for the journey of your time of transition.

Three key hallmarks—*task*, *training*, and *time*—differentiate transitional ministry from other specialized ministries. The *task* is the work that must be done to respond to the change. This work prepares the congregation for a future which will be different than previously imagined because of the change. Bridges's definitions, noted above, tell us that this task will center around the necessity of letting go of the old and moving ahead to a new reality. Sometimes we humans have a tendency to rush ahead to the next new thing, without attending to feelings, our own or others. We want to fix the situation quickly and be back to "normal" life. I believe that failure to plan for the task of transition can be a plan for failure. Once we have the task before us, the next component of transitional ministry is *training*. The wisdom and experience of the trained transitional pastor or transitional consultant is needed to guide the congregation in their work. *Time*, the final component, gives a clear signal to the congregation that there is a specific task to be done and limited time in which to accomplish this work. So let's look more closely at the three "Ts" of transitional ministry.

Task is the first component of this ministry. Some change occurs that places the congregation in transition. This change is large enough that its impact is obvious to all. Here I must add a word of caution. There are some situations in which the change itself is not known or understood, only the results. For example, for no readily apparent reason, the church has become a place of cliques and conflict. In spite of a lack of obvious cause, something has changed to move the congregation into the ambivalence of transition. The immediate goal will be to discover the cause or causes.

In traditional interim ministry, this change was always the departure of the pastor. Experience taught the church that immediately calling a new clergy person was often a formula for disaster. I often use the imperfect metaphor of marriage to explain this. When a married person becomes single—whether due to divorce or death —immediate remarriage is ill advised. The newly single person has to grieve the loss of the marriage and then acquire a new identity as a "solo." Popular radio psychologist Dr. Joy Browne refers to this as the "one-year rule." She tells her listeners, no new relationships until at least one year has passed.[5] While I do not want to imply that the priest marries the parish, this bit of pop psychology makes sense for all kinds of relationships. As Loren Mead describes in the foreword to this book, the truth of this wisdom led the Alban Institute and the Interim Ministry Network to develop a whole approach to use this time to prepare for the future.[6]

Traditionally, interim ministry refers to ministry during the time between pastors. The trained intentional interim comes to a congregation for a specified time to help the congregation work on both past and present issues so that it may prepare for the future and the arrival of a new pastor. Typically, this can be accomplished in about one year. Nancy Miller writes of the specialized work of interim ministry in chapter 3. Occasionally the pastor leaves because of misconduct, and then the interim issues are different. The specialized services of an "after pastor" are required. Barry Miller will describe this in chapter 11.

Certainly departure of a pastor is a major change, but it is not the only change that precipitates transition within a congregation. In August 2005, Hurricane Katrina's fury changed Gulf Coast churches forever. Recovery from this devastation is still ongoing today. In chapter 9, Ben Helmer describes his work with the Episcopal Diocese of Louisiana as it struggled to cope with transition.

Changes are not always due to departure or disaster. A church may find that growth has changed the character of the congregation. What was once a small to medium pastor-centered church is now overflowing with people. The structures, both physical and organizational, cannot handle the demands being placed on them. The congregation needs to move past the difficult "200 barrier," but the pastor and people do not have the skills or experience to move ahead. Expert help is needed.[7]

Sometimes change occurs slowly. Busy lives keep people from realizing that the neighborhood has changed. Most in the congregation are driving in from the suburbs for Sunday worship. The drive gets longer and harder; attendance drops. Finally the leadership understands their context has changed and they must change too. Implicit in each of these changes is the possibility of a new future. The task of transitional ministry is to prepare for that future.

Training is the second component of transitional ministry. In the twenty-first century, most clergy receive formal training prior to ordination. When I was in seminary, the classes were primarily theoretical (history, theology, and liturgy). They gave me a good theoretical foundation for the practice of ministry. Field education was where book learning was put into practice. I imagine that most clergy who went to traditional seminaries found themselves, as did

I, woefully ill-equipped for the practical reality of parish life. My real training in the praxis of ministry came from the good people of St. Matthew's Episcopal Church in Raytown, Missouri. They encouraged me to turn a head filled with theology into action. They were patient as I learned to deal with each new situation. In time each pastor learns, as I did, how to minister in a congregation. Both book knowledge and life experience teach us what we need to know. Most clergy work diligently and faithfully to the best of their ability. But when things change, most of us are not equipped to respond to the extraordinary things that happen in transition. William Bridges points out that people "expect to move straight from the old to the new. But this isn't a trip from one side of the street to the other. It's a journey from one identity to the other and that takes time."[8] The resulting heightened emotions mean that transition is a difficult time for on-the-job training of the new cleric.

Even those of us who are comfortable with change and transition in daily life may falter when our church is in transition. We remember the words "Jesus Christ is the same yesterday and today and for ever" (Hebrews 13:8) and mistakenly apply them to the church. Frantic efforts to return to equilibrium exacerbate the situation. Content people become anxious. Help is needed. Training gives the transition minister the tools to respond to such anxiety. Dr. Murray Bowen's family system theory as interpreted by Rabbi Edwin Friedman is a rich resource for this work. While Friedman's *Generation to Generation* (The Guilford Press, 1985) is a standard seminary text, most clergy need additional training before they can incorporate the theory into their practice.

The nature of the transition task determines the specific training needed. Some kinds of training provide an understanding of human interactions that gives the transitional minister a perspective from which to operate. Family system theory, which teaches the dynamics of interpersonal relationships and appreciative inquiry, which will be described in chapter 7, are examples. Other skills such as conflict resolution, strategic planning, and advanced pastoral care are generally helpful but may be more or less important depending on the task. Still other training such as fund-raising and size transition are useful for specific circumstances.[9]

This kind of practical training is usually not part of traditional seminary education. It is unfair to expect an ordained person to be expert in these specialized areas. Nevertheless, the need is great. The good news is that there are women and men who do have understanding of these special topics through both training and experience. These are the people to call upon when a church is in transition. The final section of this book provides some resources for finding trained transitional ministers.

Time is the third component of transitional ministry. In the Episcopal Church, the position of rector is tenured. While we know that our clergy come and go, the emotional and spiritual ties that are often part of the relationships between priest and people make departures problematic. Consequently the leave-taking of the rector can be laden with disappointment. Voices are heard saying things like "We thought you were here forever—don't you love us?" When I left a church because my husband had taken a new position in another state, one person's anguish was reported to me. She believed that I should have divorced my husband to remain at her church!

In contrast to the settled cleric, the transitional minister begins planning departure on day one. The letter of agreement, as Ken Ornell and I will describe more fully in chapter 4, defines the terms and tasks of the transition period and always includes a time period in which this work is to be done. The judicatory, congregation leaders, and the pastor are partners in designing the letter of agreement and therefore partners in determining the time limit. The congregation knows the terms of the letter of agreement. It is clear to all that the pastor is at First Church for a specific reason (the task) and will leave at the end of a specific time. It is possible to amend the time limit, leaving slightly earlier or later than originally planned. However, it is important that the transitional minister does not become the settled pastor. "Auditioning" for the position of the next settled pastor and preparing the congregation for a future that will include the new settled pastor are mutually exclusive. The transitional cleric's responsibility is to coach the congregation in a process of exploration that will prepare them for the future. It is not to insure that this future includes a particular person.

The time limit also helps maintain focus on the task at hand.

Any pastor knows that there is a very real sense in which the work is never done. In every interim position in which I have served, there was always the potential to do more. The profile document that serves as a letter of introduction to potential new pastors can always be a bit better; the website can use more refining. These are the work of the congregation, not the interim pastor. However, the pastor points out needs and then motivates and encourages the people in their work. We must remember that perfection is not our goal. To paraphrase the Prayer of Confession in the Episcopal Church's Book of Common Prayer, there are things to be done during transition and things to be left undone.

Any major deviation from this plan means that all partners need to revisit the situation. However, it can also mean that the next step in the life of the congregation will be different than initially imagined when the change occurred. I experienced this when I was serving a small urban church. The rector had retired and I had gone to the church as a traditional interim. During the time of this rector's service, the church had experienced slow but steady change. I was told to expect a small but busy church with an active outreach ministry and a significant local presence. I found a group of tired and dispirited people who were trying to maintain large empty buildings. Revitalizing the place and creating new identity—traditional interim goals—were beyond the possibility of the time limitations of my agreement. I realized that a long-term transition would be important but that was not what I was called to do. My charge was to prepare the church for their next settled rector. This person would lead them through the larger process of transition. The time limit helped me to keep my priorities straight, to focus on the task at hand—preparation for the new pastor—and to avoid getting caught up in trying to solve problems which were beyond the scope of my agreement.

Several years ago I was in a process of discerning a call to serve as interim rector of a program-size church. Both the vestry and the bishop told me I would be needed for two years. I could not understand the reason for the lengthy interim—there was no misconduct and no other evident large issue. Knowing that my first task would be to discern what was going on, I accepted the call. Upon my arrival I discovered a fairly peaceful congregation except when the church school was mentioned. Faces would get red, hands clenched —clearly there was an issue. I discovered that the school's rapid growth had strained resources. The governing structure did not meet the needs. Everybody was angry and no one knew how to "fix it." The pastor's departure allowed the problem, which had been quietly and slowly escalating, to surface. The school became the elephant in the room, present but not acknowledged. The unusual time period designated for this interim was the key that alerted me to look for a hidden issue.

In the summer of 2007, the Rev. Melford (Bud) Holland, director of the Episcopal Church's Office of Ministry Development, agreed to have lunch with me. I wanted to meet with Bud as I knew him to be a wise person with broad experience and understanding of the church. I hoped that Bud could explain to me why there were so many misconceptions about interim ministry. I have to confess that I wanted to fix things. The conversation was discouraging. Bud told me that there is much confusion about transitional ministry in the Episcopal Church. In some places, untrained persons serve as interim, and a few even stay on as the settled pastor, in complete disavowal of the principles of interim ministry. He stressed that there are bishops and deployment officers who do not understand the benefits of trained interim clergy. I knew Bud was right. I still felt the sting of a bishop's canon who once told me "this diocese has never had a church so sick that we needed an interim." The medical model is not helpful. But if a health model must be used, just as there are times when we need doctors and hospitals, most of us want to avoid the emergency room at all costs. I prefer to turn to preventive medicine and look at transitional ministry as a check-up to insure continued good health. This book is a direct result of my conversation with Bud. My notes from the lunch conversation were filled with questions that Bud posed. This volume is an attempt to answer the questions. The chapter titles come from the questions that Bud and I discussed in that lunch conversation.

Interim ministry came into being as a specialized ministry because of a very real need that not only still exists but is greater than ever. Churches facing the turmoil of denominational struggles, churches whose buildings have been destroyed by disaster, and churches that need to adapt to a changing environment have joined the ranks of those needing the specialized service of the trained intentional interim. In spite of such needs, there are many who are unaware of the resources that trained intentional transitional ministers can bring to these kinds of situations. As the conversation with the aforementioned canon indicates, there is a belief that interim clergy are useful only in situations where "something bad" has happened. Yes, there are times where the medical model is correct. However, it is the intention of this book to demonstrate that the scope of transitional ministry is much larger.

In 1998, Roger Nicholson edited *Temporary Shepherds* (Alban Institute, 1998), which has been an invaluable resource for traditional interim ministry. I have used this book extensively and encourage all church leaders to use it during a traditional interim ministry. It serves as an excellent guide to the work of the congregation during the interim time. *Calling Clergy* by Elizabeth Geitz (Church Publishing, 2007) is another important tool for the traditional interim time. Geitz gives a proven guide to the search process for congregations to use in the process of calling a new pastor. This book does not try to replicate either of these efforts. Because the goal here is to provide a broad frame of reference to assist congregations in transition, I suggest that effective use of this book would begin prior to consulting *Temporary Shepherds* or *Calling Clergy*. For example, in chapter 2 John Keydel gives an invaluable guide to the key steps to take after change has taken place and the congregation is in the very first stages of transition. This book is meant to be a practical and easy-to-use handbook for any person who wants to know more about ministry during transition.

As a person who trains clergy in various faith groups in interim ministry, I know the needs of transition are not limited to a given denomination. In chapter 10, Ineke Mitchell writes of her experience in the United Church of Christ where the polity presents both opportunity and obstacle to transitional ministry. The Presbyterians and the Southern Baptists have devoted resources to the training of clergy and consultants in interim ministry, as referred to in the resource section. In chapter 12, Larry Hand shows that Lutherans have made great strides in providing organizations to support interim ministry. Denominational differences are not barriers to sharing resources in this specialized ministry. Transitional ministry presents an excellent way to work ecumenically.

All of the chapter authors are experienced transitional ministers. Each will describe a particular area of transitional ministry in which he or she has expertise. They will use language that comes out of their particular faith tradition. To help the reader interpret the various position titles, there is a list of comparable terms for each denomination in the resource section. Most of the chapter authors have served in the role of traditional interim. However, as more congregations and clergy come to understand transition as a time of opportunity, trained consultants and clergy will bring their special skills and experience to increasingly varied situations.

I imagine that need brought many of you to this book. If you are reading these words, you probably have had some experience of change in your church and want to know what to do next. Perhaps you are a judicatory leader who has heard various conflicting reports about interim ministry. Maybe you are a clergy person who is thinking about becoming trained in this specialized work. Or perhaps you are the leader of a synagogue who is exploring how to respond to transition in your own setting. Whoever you are, you want to know more.

You may choose to read this book from front to back, but it does not need to be read this way. You may want to go right to that chapter which responds to your issue of the moment. Perhaps the resource section meets your needs right now and you will return to the various chapters later as need arises. It is our intention to have current relevant information on the book's page on the Church Publishing website (www.churchpublishing.org/transitionalministry).

Our faith story tells us that transition has been a time of tremendous growth for the people of God. The exodus and the forty years of wilderness wandering are prime examples. The departure of the Hebrews through the parted waters of the Red Sea is the change event. The former inhabitants of Egypt are now in the Sinai desert. Their external circumstances have changed. During the forty years of their transition, they moaned and complained but finally learned to trust God. The time of transition formed this grumbling group of former slaves into a community of faith. Like a good interim pastor, Moses helped the Hebrews use their wilderness time to prepare them to enter the Promised Land.

Fast-forward from the Sinai to Jerusalem and the very first Easter. The entire Easter season celebrated by the Christian church is a traditional interim ministry. The pastor (Jesus) has left. The Risen Christ comes to be with the disciples to help them prepare for the "one who is to come"—the Holy Spirit. As an interim pastor, I have found that the Easter season lectionary texts illuminate the process and tasks of the interim time. In the resource section I have included a sermon that I preached at All Saints' Episcopal Church in Jacksonville, Florida, with this goal in mind.

Indeed, our faith tradition is emphatic about transition as a time rich with potential for growth and preparation for the future. We have often missed this focus. Somehow in our desperation to reach the destination we have forgotten the value of the journey. This book is an effort to reclaim this forgotten treasure.

Change and transition will continue to be part of church life. As in all of life, each of us has a choice to make about how we will respond to change within the church. Transition can be a time of hope and optimism. I hope that this book will inspire you and give you tools to use as you respond to transition.

Notes

1. Bob Dylan, "*The Times They Are a-Changin'.*" Special Rider Music, 1963, 1991.

2. "Kübler-Ross model." Wikipedia, http://en.wikipedia.org/wiki/Kubler-Ross_model (accessed February 8, 2009).

3. William Bridges, *Managing Transitions: Making the Most of Change* (Reading, MA: Perseus Books, 1991), 3.

4. Ibid., 4., emphasis added.

5. Wikepedia gives this information about Dr. Joy: "**Dr. Joy Browne** (born 1944) is a radio psychologist. She is a licensed clinical psychologist whose syndicated show is the longest-running call-in therapy show in the

United States. Her show originates from radio station WOR (AM) (New York City). Browne is also known for her 'one-year rule,' which states that people who have lost a spouse or partner due to break-up, death or divorce should wait at a minimum one year before resuming romantic relationships." "Joy Browne." Wikipedia, http://en.wikipedia.org/wiki/Joy_Browne (accessed February 8, 2009).

6. See the resource section for other approaches to interim ministry.

7. For information on this topic, see Alice Mann, *The in-Between Church: Navigating Size Transitions In Congregations* (Herndon, VA: Alban Institute, 1998).

8. Bridges, *Managing Transitions*, 37.

9. See the resource section for information about training.

Chapter 2

WHAT DO WE DO FIRST?

John Keydel

Since 2000, I have had the pleasure and privilege of being a full-time practitioner of the art that the Episcopal Church is increasingly referring to as "transition ministry." While they are often still referred to as diocesan deployment officers, I work with colleagues throughout the Episcopal Church and with interdenominational organizations like the Interim Ministry Network (IMN) to help guide congregations and their members through the changes that inevitably come into the life of every congregation. During these years, I have learned that few events in the life of any organization hold as much potential for deep and lasting change as the announcement of the imminent departure of a congregation's senior cleric. Regardless of the reason for the resignation—retirement, acceptance of another call or appointment, economics, misconduct, or whatever else—the members of a congregation suddenly find themselves face-to-face with the sudden reality of unexpected change. The process of dealing with change is often referred to as transition. It almost always involves a deep reconsideration of many familiar ways of doing things, as well as the occasional rediscovery and certain reinterpretation of the familiar old stories. For the congregational leadership, whether elected or appointed, this combination of change and transition has an eerie sense of being tossed out into the unknown. My favorite singer-songwriter, Carrie Newcomer, expresses this feeling wonderfully: "What used to be sure up and walked out the door, and the old ways I knew just don't work anymore."[1]

I view the announcement of the imminent departure of a senior cleric as a wonderfully complex, often bittersweet opportunity to engage a congregation in a unique series of strategic conversations. These conversations usually unfold over a period of weeks and months. They are both formal and informal, and they involve the members of the congregation, its governing body (vestry, session,

15

board, etc.), and especially the officers of that body. For convenience, I will follow Episcopal nomenclature and refer to the governing body as the vestry, and the person(s) who wear the mantle of elected leadership as warden.[2]

Because the resignation of a cleric is often experienced as sudden and immediate, this chapter focuses on the emergent conversations that take place in the very earliest parts of the transition process, before an intentional interim is engaged. In addition to providing the information that makes the smooth facilitation of strategic decisions even possible, these conversations also serve as concrete expressions of the development of the crucial relationship between the congregational leadership and the transition specialist at the judicatory (diocese, synod, conference, etc.) level. This relationship is fundamental to a smooth transition, and is a clear expression of the belief that judicatory structures and personnel exist to assist the bishop in the development of the ministry of each congregation and its members—guiding, supporting, and setting the tone and direction of many of the working relationships that will follow. Not surprisingly, this relationship takes on particular importance any time a congregation finds itself being swept into the currents of transition.

As soon as the departing cleric has formally announced his or her intention to resign, I get in touch with the warden(s). Some have called me even before the formal announcement has been made. Regardless of who initiates it, I see this conversation having two main purposes. The first, and most important, is to begin to expand and further develop whatever working relationship that we may already have, acknowledge the dramatically expanded responsibilities that have fallen to them in light of the clergy resignation, and make sure that they really do know that they really can (and should!) call or e-mail me whenever they encounter unforeseen situations or questions.

The second purpose is to arrange for a special meeting of the vestry. This meeting is primarily informational—anticipating, addressing, and informing emerging questions and concerns that, for the most part, have not been even thought of, let alone articulated. By virtue of the way that the conversation is conducted, it can work at many other levels, and can do much to set the tone for the journey of transition that began with the clergy resignation. Because the transition process impacts every aspect of the life of the entire congregation, I have a very strong preference for this meeting to take place on a Sunday and to be open to any and all members of the congregation. It is also very important that this meeting include the departing cleric, whenever possible. While s/he and I will have already discussed this, their presence—while perhaps a bit awkward or uncomfortable for some —adds an essential recognition of the reality of the change that is the reason for the meeting.

The special meeting (usually lasting around ninety minutes) might be understood as the convergence of a wide array of topics and concerns; some carrying a clear and present sense of immediacy, others simply outline and prefigure material that will become important much later in the journey. Above all, the meeting is intended to set an important attitudinal and emotional tone for the journey ahead, and to do so publicly, at the very beginning of the journey.

At the most basic level, this meeting often provides the first occasion for the public naming of their situation, and further allows me to be a present and incarnate witness to the reality of that situation. "I guess things really are changing; after all, the deployment officer is here for a special meeting!" Without a clear naming of the situation and its explicit acknowledgement, denial or fear-based deferral of the change that has ushered in the new reality can often continue to be a very powerful, even dominant, force. By recognizing and acknowledging what's actually happening within the congregation, we also accept that anxiety is and will continue to be present. My favorite definition of anxiety is that which arises out of the gap between what is and what could be, a gap that most of us are astonishingly creative in filling. We also recognize that this sense of anxiety will be expressed in different ways, at different times, by different people, and to affirm that all of this is a normal expression of a system in transition. Indeed, I make a point to note that it really is OK—in fact, I worry if it doesn't happen.

Another important aspect of this meeting is the tangible fact of my own presence and witness among them; to model well-differentiated leadership, especially for the formal leadership of the congregation. In a separate meeting, I remind the vestry that part of leadership is acknowledging the reality that the rest of the congregation will automatically look to their leadership example. If they are flustered and short-tempered, it's going to be a rough ride and they should start issuing life vests and helmets. But if they are relaxed and confident, most of the congregation will be quite happy to follow their leadership. By simply being present to and with them as they encounter many of the unexpected realities of being in transition, I provide a tangible way of letting them know that there is someone in the judicatory office (in addition to the bishop) who can usually answer their questions, help clarify misunderstandings and adjudicate disagreements, explain policies and procedures, and walk with them on their journey.

Much of the actual content of the special meeting is devoted to a broad outline of the journey of transition, drawing particular attention to the various options and decision points, conveying in the clearest terms possible that what I am presenting is a general *description*, not a *prescription*. The day of the "one size fits all" transition process is long gone; instead, we are interested in doing whatever we can to empower them to articulate and be the Body of Christ at this particular time and in this particular place. While there are certainly common processes, and while we may borrow elements from the large church up the road, or the family-sized church across town, we are primarily concerned with doing effective ministry in the unique context of this particular congregation. Having said that, I also hasten to point out that everything that takes place in the "standard process" happens for at least one very good reason, and I can usually tell very specific stories about congregations that did (and did not) choose to observe any specific steps. In my experience, it is very important to make sure that they know that they do have both options and limitations, and to begin to be clear about what some of those might be. While it is probably not desirable or possible to work out all the options and details immediately, it is important to have the leaders and the members of the congregation leave the meeting with at least some sense of confident familiarity with the shape of the overall process. In recognition of the fact that different people absorb and process information in different ways and at different rates, and that some people like to take notes, I generally provide a graphic map or a flowchart as a handout. An example is in the resource section.

A further important purpose of the meeting is to model and encourage a spirit of open questioning and responsive communication. The free and easy availability of every kind of information does much to prevent (or at least limit) the spread of rumors or conspiracy theories. This is achieved by structuring the flow and tone of the overall experience in such a way that as many people as possible hear the same thing at the same time in the same words, and have ample opportunity to ask any and every kind of question.

At some point during the conversation, the question of diocesan, or judicatory, assistance always arises. This is an important part of the clear and honest depiction of their overall context, and may well have a significant impact on later decisions. It is important to let them know what resources are (experience, guidance, expertise) and are not (extensive financial resources) available from the judicatory, as well as whatever limitations and requirements might apply. The type of available resources will vary widely among denominations and local judicatories.

While some will certainly need to be reminded later, the special meeting is also an opportunity to point to the many phases, the many options, and the vast amount of just plain work that will need to be done in the coming months, and to acknowledge that all of this takes time for work, prayer, and discernment if it is to be done well. Especially in a corporate type of congregation, a pointed comparison is frequently made to the business world, questioning the length of time that the church's process seems to take. The simplest answer is that most healthy and dynamic businesses engage in ongoing and comprehensive processes of strategic planning that include detailed succession planning at almost every level of the organization. For a wide variety of reasons, this can be said of very few congregations.

Another important purpose of the special meeting is to begin to identify and clarify the many different role boundaries, expectations, and limitations that apply to intentional interim clergy, supply clergy, paid employees, volunteers, and the members and officers of the vestry and search committee. It is often of the utmost importance to state—publicly, clearly, unequivocally, and occasionally repeatedly—who does (and equally, who does not) do what, and to what extent, during the transition. Generally, clergy oversee things liturgical and pastoral, while the members of the elected leadership are responsible for the physical and fiscal fabric of the congregation. Programming usually requires collaboration between clergy and appointed laity. In congregations where this area is effectively addressed at the beginning, over-functioning, controlling, or autocratic behavior is far less likely to emerge later on, and if it should arise, the fact of the public precedent usually makes it far easier to deal with.

Of far greater tenderness, especially when the departing cleric is planning to remain in the area, or has been in place more than ten or twelve years, is the need to explain, in a way that is both pastorally sensitive and utterly clear, that he or she has in fact resigned, and, as a result, will not be available for any funerals, weddings, or baptisms without the explicit and event-specific permission of the bishop. This is also an appropriate time to note the bishop's expectation that he or she will remove themselves from the congregation's informal communication processes known as the "gossip circuit" or the "coconut telegraph." The opportunity to do this in public, and in the presence of the departing cleric, is one of the principal reasons that she or he should be at the meeting. Ideally, the departing cleric will also take proactive responsibility for the clear articulation and observation of these boundaries; some have even discussed them in a letter to the members of the congregation.

Closely related to the functional absence of the former pastor is the inevitable anxiety about emergency pastoral coverage. All I can say here is that, in all probability, something of an emergency or unexpected nature will happen, and that the leadership of the congregation, working together with local clergy and judicatory staff, will make sure that unexpected pastoral emergencies are addressed effectively and with dignity and grace. While occasionally a bit harrowing, the experience of actually doing so can be a powerful witness to the effectiveness of the congregation and its non ordained leadership.

After the conversations about boundaries, a shift of attention to some form of present-focused action is usually perceived as a breath of fresh air. There are important things to be done, and they need to be done soon. Perhaps the most important is for the congregation and its leadership to claim and celebrate the ministry that they have had with the departing cleric. Almost regardless of the stated reasons for the resignation, almost regardless of the length and quality of the tenure, there has been important shared ministry. Lives have begun and ended; important ministry has been done; faith has been deepened; joys and sorrows have been shared. All of this needs to be recalled, reacknowledged, and celebrated. Both the congregation and the departing cleric will be rewarded, strengthened, and enriched by this, and all will be able to move into the next part of their journey with a renewed sense of accomplishment and closure.

Part of preparing for the departure is the need to provide closure to the events or processes of the past. It is important that each person, speaking the truth in love, say what needs to be said to the departing cleric; this is especially true of those things that are more difficult or emotionally charged. Apart from its strategic importance for the tone of the transition period, this is a prime time to exercise the ministry of reconciliation. Don't wait until the rush at the end. It's much healthier to have those conversations in person, while there's still adequate time to think, pray, and then follow up. It is also important to remember that the real goal is not ultimate resolution so much as mutually acceptable closure; it is often more difficult to agree to disagree, but it frees both people to move forward.

From an organizational and procedural point of view, it is often very important to document the many things that everyone has taken for granted for years and years. One warden referred to this as "picking the rector's brain." How do things actually get done around here? Write it all down: What? When? Who? How? and (especially) Why? In many congregations, the departing clergy may be the only person with direct working knowledge of many areas of congregational life; this is especially true with external relationships like funeral directors, contractors, or suppliers, and other area clergy. It may seem tedious at the time, but it is a wonderful way to make sure that working information is retained; and besides, it is much easier to do the Christmas pageant if someone knows where the costumes were stored last year.

When the time for good-byes draws near, the theme of celebrating common ministry takes two formal and important expressions—the farewell party and the final service. In keeping with our
identity as an Easter people, neither of these events is a funeral or a
wake, but a joyful, if poignant, celebration and recollection of years
of shared life and ministry. One congregation's farewell party took
the form of a "roast," with pointed and hilarious recollections of
various events in the ministry of the church, and even featured a
special keynote appearance by Father Guido Sarducci (actually the
senior warden), who made sure that the tears that were shed were
at least as much from sheer laughter as joyful sadness. As much as
the party is the social celebration, the importance of the ritual and
liturgical transition which is an integral part of the Service for the
Ending of a Pastoral Relationship cannot be overstated. Different
denominations and judicatories will have different approaches and
resources to apply to this, but the ritual of handing over the symbols
and instruments of the continuing ministry of the congregation to
those who will carry those ministries on is a powerful personal,
ministerial, and theological action. In the same way, the direct
involvement of judicatory personnel is an implicit guarantee of care
and continuation.

While the threads mentioned above are converging on the
special meeting and the various ending celebrations, the leadership
must turn its attention to the continuation of the congregation's
ministry. While this material is almost always outlined within the
larger meeting, it is crucial for the members of the vestry to have a
more complete understanding of what intentional interim ministry
is, and how and why it may apply in their specific situation. This
also has the significant advantage of focusing their attention on the
long-term success of the next pastorate, and beginning to call attention to the congregation's future ministry.

Over the years, I have found that the easiest avenue of entrée
is to provide a very brief narrative review of the key findings of the
Alban Institute research that gave rise to the concept of intentional
interims, and the development of the Interim Ministry Network
in the early 1980s. I augment this narrative with my own views
concerning different levels of congregational situations. As I have

written elsewhere (*IMN ReVisions,* Autumn 2007), it is useful to think of three levels of clergy presence during a time of congregational transition:

- **Level Three** or **Third Tier** exists in the wake of congregational or personal trauma, any kind of abuse or misconduct, deep conflict within the congregation, or following a very short (abandonment) or very long (over ten years) pastorate. If it is at all possible, an intentional interim with training and experience in the relevant area is essential to address these situations, and to do so before the work of transition can even begin. Fortunately these situations are relatively rare, and are almost always thoroughly and immediately self-evident.

- **Level Two** or **Second Tier** covers most intentional interim situations. The congregation is in transition, but there is no significant conflict or trauma. It is here that I outline the developmental tasks of the interim period and point out that the interim's facilitation of these tasks is in addition to all the other things that senior pastors normally do. Obviously these require clergy who have additional training and experience (and cost), but the congregational reward is a much smoother and more effective passage through the transition period and into the startup of the next pastorate.

- **Level One** or **First Tier** usually appears in times of transition as some variant on part-time or Sunday supply, possibly with an expectation to cover pastoral emergencies. This is often motivated by a desire to save money, to minimize the significance of the transition, or to avoid addressing some aspect of the mission and ministry of the congregation and its unique context. The cleric is expected to provide liturgical and pastoral support, but this is usually a part-time position, so the mantle of fiscal and physical administration, program development and implementation, mission or outreach, and the like must rest firmly on the shoulders of the congregation's lay leadership. There is usually little or no attention given to matters of transition, except as may be suggested by a search consultant or transition companion to the search committee.

Once these levels have been described to the vestry, we discuss what is most appropriate and desirable, given the congregational reality and the resources available. The engagement of an intentional interim is a financial commitment similar to, and occasionally even greater than, the support of the previous pastor. There must be a reasonable expectation that the financial resources to provide for this will be present. If this seems not to be the case, and the resources are not likely to be available (an increasingly frequent situation), our conversations shift out of the current discussion of intentional interim ministry, and move into deeper and more protracted considerations of congregational identity and development, and the future role of clergy within that congregation.

Assuming that there is a reasonable expectation of the support of a full-time intentional interim, the conversation moves to the process of identifying and engaging such a person. As a result of hard-won experience, I stress that the identification and engagement of an interim is not a compressed search process, but rather a process of serial referrals based in large part on the answers to several key questions:

> *Who will come for what we can pay?* This revisits the question of resources discussed above and allows me to further stress that intentional interim ministry is a very particular ministry specialty which requires special training, special kinds of experience, and a particular type of emotional and psychological makeup. At this point we often talk briefly about the work of the interim, especially the need to enter and exit a congregational system quickly and effectively, as well as the ability to make initial and independent assessments of the state of the congregation and its various systems. Again, all of this is in addition to the things that a "normal" senior pastor is expected to do.

Who has the skill, experience, and outlook that we need?
This question addresses the contextual realities of the congregation and its history. Matters of liturgical preference, theology, socioeconomics and politics, and educational levels are all relevant here. What we are always looking for is someone who can come into this congregation quickly and work effectively within its unique cultural and contextual reality. At this point, it is very important to stress that the interim is not there to be either the clone or the anti-clone of the last pastor. The interim is there to facilitate and guide the members and leaders of the congregation as they do the occasionally difficult work of transition. This means that, like a good coach, the interim may or may not be well-liked, popular, or non-controversial; what is most important is that the interim be effective.

How long will this take? It is extraordinarily difficult to provide precise estimates concerning the length of time that an interim will need to facilitate the transition work of the congregation. This is because of the many personal and organizational variables that may be involved. Is the congregation clearly focused on a well-known and affirmed mission? Is there serious conflict? Over what? Are the issues in the open and accessible, or are there congregational secrets and distinct and exclusive power groups? Is the leadership of the congregation skilled at resolving differences? Are the necessary resources of time, talent, and treasure readily available? The process of genuine transition is rarely accomplished in less than twelve months, and it is important to remember that a congregation that has experienced any kind of trauma cannot begin the work of transition until the trauma has been dealt with in as constructive a manner as possible. On the other hand, a transition process that takes much longer than twenty-four months is likely doing the work of specific redevelopment rather than transition.

Who is available when we need them? This is the last, and often the trickiest, question in the sequence because until we know what resources we can apply and what characteristics are necessary, it doesn't matter who's available. Once we do know those things, however, the matter of availability becomes all-important. Most intentional interims work on the basis of twelve-, eighteen-, or twenty-four-month agreements, and it is usually pointless to try to engage an interim who is just five months into an eighteen-month commitment.

An important part of my work as canon for transition ministries is to maintain ongoing relationships with skilled and experienced interims, knowing where they are currently serving, when they may be available, how much compensation they require, and what their particular skills and approaches are. Sometimes I seek them out; sometimes in the course of looking for their next position, they contact me.

In addition to my relationships with interims, I rely heavily on my relationships with my judicatory colleagues around the church. Many of us talk regularly by phone, and several formal and informal groups meet on a regular basis. Our conversations about clergy and congregations are characterized by an almost unique level of confidentiality and honesty (often to the point of being blunt). Among our more regular conversations are discussions of the work being done by the interims working in their various areas. Even when I know a particular interim well, I want to know how that work is regarded by my judicatory colleague who is currently overseeing that person's work, and why. Without the honesty and frequency of these conversations, it would be extraordinarily difficult for me to recommend an interim to a congregation. As a sidebar, this means that if you are an interim (experienced, brand new, or in-between) reading this book, you would be wise to make sure that the judicatory staff person in your area knows who and where you are and something about the work that you are currently doing. Contact information can be notoriously difficult to keep current. At the risk of being utterly obvious, if you have any sort of misunderstandings or disagreements with that person, or any other judicatory person, be sure to work them out as soon as possible.

Once I have identified and talked with a suitable interim, I urge the wardens to be in immediate contact with him or her. If they want to have an in-person meeting, that's fine, but the purpose of the meeting is not for the warden to try to "interview" the interim, but to talk about the congregation and its ministry as a way of determining whether or not the basic interpersonal chemistry is such that they can work together in an effective manner, and whether or not the context is such that the interim will "fit" that congregation. There are, after all, people who walk into the room and the hair on the back of your neck immediately stands on end; you obviously don't want to have to work closely with that person for a year. If that test works, my advice to the vestry and wardens is to work with me to engage that interim as soon as humanly possible, get the agreement into a formal letter of agreement, and get ready for the next leg of the transition!

I close this chapter just as the congregation begins to work with its new interim, in the way I began, with another line from my friend Carrie Newcomer's song "Throw Me a Line": "There's a still quiet voice, it sounds a little like mine, saying you're right where you should be, it's just gonna take time. . . ."

Wise words to recall as the work unfolds.

Notes

1. Carrie Newcomer, "Throw Me a Line," *Geography of Light*, Rounder, 2008.

2. See resource list for a chart giving comparable names for titles and positions in the various denominations.

Chapter 3

WHAT DOES AN INTERIM PASTOR DO?

Nancy Miller

What *does* an interim minister do? That is a very good question, and one that both parishioners and judicatory personnel have every business asking. What can (and should) we expect an interim to do, and what can we expect the interim *not* to do?

One particular expression destined to put a scowl on the face of a trained intentional interim pastor is this: "S/He is *just* an interim." First, it sounds and feels dismissive to the cleric, as though interim clergy are not "real" clergy. And second, it suggests that the interim time—the time of transition—is somehow not very important to a congregation.

In many traditions and in many venues, the time of transition has generally been considered as something to endure, with the hope that it will pass quickly and uneventfully. Typically, in such situations, parishes will use the services of supply clergy who will be present primarily on Sundays, but rarely otherwise. Too often, alas, parishes will bring on board a retired cleric, who will recycle sermons and be pleasant at coffee hour, but do very little else. Not surprisingly, in such situations, the time of transition is a time when attendance, giving, and energy often decline—and decline significantly.

It doesn't have to be that way.

Indeed, quite the opposite can be the case. Many parishes have been willing to embrace the transition between one pastor and the next as a time of opportunity—an opportunity right from God's heart. And those parishes, in most cases, have encountered the transition as a time of energy and growth.

To be sure, most churches need to be persuaded to engage the time of transition as a time of opportunity, and such persuasion is—or should be—the work of the judicatory staff. Unfortunately, many judicatory staff people (including bishops) aren't prepared or even willing to take on that role. In fairness, most judicatory personnel have never served in an interim capacity, so they have no first-hand experience. But the need is there, and too often it is not being met. That said, an intentional interim cleric is not the settled pastor, nor a supply priest, but quite a different entity. As an aside, and with the risk of being accused of picking nits, the term "settled" rector seems far more appropriate than "permanent" rector. No pastor is "permanent"; some tenures are simply longer than others. Let me also add that while these comments apply in particular to parishes in transition, they certainly carry over into transitional times in other settings, such as business venues or volunteer organizations.

Like the settled rector, the interim engages in all the priestly functions. S/he presides at the liturgy, preaches, teaches, baptizes, does pre-marital counseling, officiates at weddings, visits the sick, buries the dead, and comforts those who mourn. An interim attends and may well chair vestry meetings, and is also responsible for the functioning of the parish office, including the supervision of personnel, conducting performance reviews, chairing staff meetings, and over-sight of parish finances.

Most trained and intentional interim clergy feel strongly that they should serve parishes at the same "level" as the previous and future settled pastors. So, for example, if the previous rector was full-time, so too should the interim be. Similarly, a half-time rector's position would call for a half-time interim.

Like the settled rector, the interim engages the larger church by participating in events of the deanery/convocation, the diocese, ecumenical gatherings, and organizations such as the Interim Ministry Network (IMN). Even, for example, when an interim is serving in a diocese where s/he is not canonically resident, s/he attends diocesan convention, often (though not always) as a non-voting participant. To be sure, an interim priest who is serving in town or state that is not "home" may well not engage the community as fully as the settled rector. For example, the interim may well choose not to join the local Rotary Club.

That said, however, intentional interims take on tasks that most settled clergy do not even approach. The IMN has identified important work for a congregation to accomplish during the time of transition. This work is generally described by the IMN as the five developmental tasks and the seven process tasks. Intentional interim clergy are trained to lead a parish through the developmental and process tasks. Without attempting to offer a full training program in one short chapter, let me expand a bit on these tasks.

The five developmental tasks are essentially the work of the congregation. It is the responsibility of the interim to guide the congregation through these tasks:

- Examining the history of the parish and coming to terms with the past;

- Claiming the current identity of the parish;

- Encouraging new leadership (while still valuing the old leadership);

- Renewing and strengthening the relationship with the diocese;

- Preparing to welcome the new rector.

The first developmental task is coming to terms with history. As my ninth-grade history teacher used to quote often: "Those who don't know their history are doomed to repeat it," and I am convinced that she was correct. The point of examining a parish's history is not to pass judgment one way or the other, but rather to name it honestly so that the parish can make an informed and prayerful decision about how to move forward. In one parish in transition, the interim followed decades of alleged clergy sexual misconduct. All the facts will never be fully known because most of the players are no longer around, and some are no longer alive. But what the parish came to recognize, as the parishioners were willing to examine their history, was that they could have been more active in halting this behavior. To their great credit, parishioners were willing to claim their role in the tragedy, in the interest of its never happening again.

Developmental task two is claiming the current identity. Put bluntly, this is not your grandmother's church. One particular congregation comes to mind that would currently be considered "inner city." But years ago, when the lines between urban and suburban were much less clear (at least in this particular city), it was a church that felt very different, with many generations of its families coming to church from far and wide. The good leadership in that parish named the change and took the opportunity to begin a children's choir. As they had hoped—and to their great delight —it was the children's presence at the parish than encouraged their parents (and grandparents) to come to church with them. And then the parish could legitimately claim its current identity as a family-friendly urban congregation.

The third developmental task is encouraging new leadership. Parishes tend to cling to leaders, especially those who tackle their work with joy and competence. And rightly so. But we tend to turn leadership roles into life sentences. I have often shared with parishes my particular dream that *every* lay leadership ministry in a parish would be well-served to have term limits. The positive effects of such a protocol are several. First, when the term limit is up, leaving the position is in no way a comment about the work that has (or hasn't) been accomplished. Second, it encourages parishioners to think and pray about what God might like to see them do next. And finally, it spreads the wealth, because more parishioners become involved. People even discover that they have gifts and passions that they hadn't previously claimed.

Developmental task four is renewing and strengthening the relationship with the diocese. How many times have I heard parishioner comment about "those people" who labor in diocesan offices: "Well, what have *they done for us lately?*" More often than not, parishioners see what the parish contributes to the diocesan budget but don't see what return comes back to the parish. In fairness, much of the work done by bishops and other diocesan staff members is, of necessity, not visible to the diocese at large. But in a time of transition in a parish, there is great opportunity for working together happily and productively. If nothing else, the work of diocesan personnel in the search for the new pastor is visible, helpful, and positive.

The fifth developmental task is preparing to welcome the new pastor. My usual approach to this task is to invite the formation of a short-term committee that I call C.H.O.R.U.S.—the Committee to

Help Our (new) Rector Understand Stuff. This is a committee that can gather whatever is necessary to help the new rector (and family) feel settled and "at home" as quickly as possible. Such efforts can include everything from finding a real estate agent to offering tips on where to shop and where to vote.

While the developmental tasks usually begin with examining history and end with preparing to welcome the new rector, they are not sequential. In fact, most often, all are being addressed at the same time. How do we know if sufficient attention has been given to the developmental tasks? The proof always shows in the congregation's profile. While the actual production of the profile is usually overseen by the search consultant, not the interim pastor, the content should be a reflection of the shared ministry of pastor and people. This document is meant to be a fair and accurate description of the parish as it is now and as it hopes to be in the future. Does the profile tell the truth or does it hide the truth?

A colleague recently showed me a profile which clearly demonstrated that the congregation had done its work. The church in question was in the unhappy situation of living with a deficit budget. This is not the kind of thing that will be attractive to clergy who are candidates for the settled position. Nevertheless, this church wanted to show their hard-won honesty and that they do not expect the new cleric to "fix" their problems. The resulting document is a beautiful testament to their transparency and to their commitment to their own ministry, as this section shows:

> First Church has been operating at a deficit in recent years, with the deficits being offset by liquidation of endowment funds. We have cut the deficit by nearly one-half in 2007 over the preceding year, and the projected 2008 deficit is 30% less than that of 2007. Our staff and leadership council continue to work hard to further reduce our deficit.

> The deficits took time to develop and were the result of a number of factors; reversing this course will take time. However, the leadership council has begun to make changes in the budget and stewardship processes aimed at improving our fiscal course and putting First Church on a more sound

financial footing. Beginning in 2008, the budget process will have the chairs of the clusters and committees develop budgets for their programs, rather than having the leadership council develop budgets for them. This process will give the chairs and the committees more ownership, and therefore responsibility, for their budgets with the goal of improved fiscal management.

On the pledging and giving side of the equation, the leadership council is in the process of developing a year-round stewardship program. While the development process has been slow, and such a program has not fully caught on with the congregation, we believe some progress has been made. We look forward to working with our new pastor to continue that progress as we work toward a more stable financial future.[1]

The process tasks are the work of the interim and focus on the "process" as opposed to the content (e.g., preaching) of the interim's work. These tasks are:

- Joining

- Connecting

- Focusing

- Analyzing

- Assuming responsibility

- Evaluation

- Exiting

Interim clergy are especially conscious of and attentive to the "process tasks," which are important both for the interim pastor and for the parish as a whole. Without going into minute detail, let me offer some examples.

Joining and connecting. One striking difference between settled and interim clergy is the reality that interims have to "hit the ground running," which is the origin of one common nickname for an interim priest: the "faster pastor." Even though their tenure is by definition limited in duration, interim clergy cannot refrain from committing themselves to the parish and connecting fully. Interims simply must let themselves fall in love with the congregation, despite the reality that the task of saying good-bye is always right around the corner.

Focusing. The time of transition provides a particular opportunity to invite the lay people of the parish to claim "ownership" of the parish as theirs. There is a bishop of the church (who will remain anonymous) who bristles whenever he hears a priest refer to a congregation as "my" parish. The parish is, after all, Christ's church, not ours, which is certainly true. There is a tendency, however, for lay persons to cede responsibility for the life and activity of the parish to the rector.

Analyzing. The time of transition is also a wonderful time to put issues of ownership into healthy perspective. In that spirit, it is an opportune moment to articulate current vision and direction for the parish. Ideally, this is an ongoing task in every parish, whether in transition or not. The reality, however, is that seasons of transition are the times when parishioners are most willing to engage that task, and interims can be most helpful in this endeavor, especially since they can be objective, not having previously been part of the parish.

I am reminded of one church in transition where one member expressed the fear that the parish would call yet another rector who would come and "lay a vision" on the parish. That was a golden moment for the interim to suggest that part of the role of the parish leadership is to help the parish articulate its current vision, with the hoped-for result that the new settled rector would be invited to help lead the parish toward that vision.

Assuming responsibility and evaluating. Like settled clergy, interim clergy are often confronted by conflict within the parish. As is the case in settled situations, avoidance of conflict serves neither the parish nor the Gospel. It often happens that the clergy person —settled or interim—becomes the focus of parishioners' anxiety and anger, and the challenge is to distinguish between legitimate criticism and anxiety that is simply aimed at the cleric. Such distinction serves well in dealing with these two process tasks: assuming responsibility and evaluating.

One true story illustrates the different roles of settled and transitional clergy and provides a good example of evaluating. It occurred toward the beginning of the time of transition. The parish had been well-served for several years by a rector who had then accepted another call. The interim arrived, and the parish soon discovered the meaning of the term "leadership style." The leadership style of the interim was noticeably different than that of the former rector. The previous rector was nothing if not laid-back. That is emphatically not a euphemism for "lazy," but laid-back was indeed that priest's style. The interim, by contrast, was high energy personified, and heard himself described as a "whirling dervish." One style wasn't necessarily better than the other, but they were indeed different.

By the time the interim had been in place for a few months, the parish had come to appreciate the gifts that he brought to the parish. At a vestry meeting, the interim observed that the parish had indeed experienced two diverse styles of leadership. The interim also suggested that it was the task of the parish leadership (and, in particular, the vestry) to contemplate what particular leadership style might be most helpful and appropriate as the parish moved into the next chapter of its life as the Body of Christ in that particular place and at that particular time. That interim even volunteered to try to model different leadership styles for the parish if they would find that helpful.

In another parish, one which had moved rather suddenly into transition, the liturgical habit included chanting by the priest at certain times during worship. Their interim, however, did not have the gift of singing. What the parish experienced during the time of transition was not only the recognition that worship could happen —and happily—without the priest singing, but they also came to appreciate that they really did prefer a "sung" service and were able to articulate the hope and expectation that the called rector would indeed bring that gift.

Exiting. Finally, saying good-bye—for interims as well as settled clergy—is wrenching, and interims can set a helpful example to parishes by leaving gracefully and definitely. This last task can be particularly important in congregations which have negative experiences surrounding a priest's departure.

As mentioned earlier, a reality that is particular to intentional interim ministry is that bishops and their staff are—alas—generally not especially conversant in or even aware of the specific opportunities and the challenges of ministry in times of transition, since most have never served in such a capacity. Also, many look on the parish transition as a time to avoid confrontation. The time of transition is not a time to avoid conflict. Quite the opposite, in fact. Why should the new settled priest inherit a situation of conflict about which s/he knows nothing and had no part in creating?

During such times, the relationship between the interim and the bishop and diocesan staff is vitally important, especially if the parish is in the midst of conflict. Sadly, when bishops and judicatory staff members avoid conflict, they often do not know how to interpret complaints about interim clergy. Sometimes the complaints are legitimate. But there are times when the most flattering comment about interim priests is that the parishes they serve complain about them for all the right reasons. One translation of that comment would be that the interims are indeed tackling all the issues.

Interim clergy, for the most part, have a clause in the letters of agreement that states clearly that they may not be considered for the settled position. This qualifies as best practice for a number of reasons. First, if the interim is eligible to be a candidate for the settled position, the playing field among candidates is inherently uneven. But also, if the interim priest is both serving as the interim and "auditioning" for the job, s/he may shy away from confronting the tough issues.

One parish in transition was in significant conflict about a particular outreach project which had been started some years before. One area of conflict was whether the project should continue or whether its effectiveness was essentially a thing of the past. But an even more important issue was how the people who had been engaged in the project felt underappreciated and badly treated. A deep rift had developed, and the two sides could barely speak. Most of the conversations about the project were happening in the parking lot, rather than face-to-face. The interim, over many months, helped that situation change. The project was indeed halted, but the parties were talking with each other, rather than about each other —and with civility, too.

Interim clergy are not engaged in bringing about change for its own sake. Rather, they are engaged in helping congregations acknowledge and embrace the reality that change happens and then helping them embrace changes that they discern are of God.

Interim ministry is not diametrically different from settled ministry, but the challenges are indeed qualitatively different. Hence the need for trained, committed, and intentional interim clergy who are appreciated and supported by their bishops.

Note

1. Names have been changed to protect the privacy of the congregation.

Chapter 4

WHY HAVE A LETTER OF AGREEMENT?

KEN ORNELL AND MOLLY DALE SMITH

A letter of agreement is more than a document concerning compensation. It is here that the focus of the interim time and the appropriate responsibilities are defined. Expectations on the part of the cleric and parish leadership are specific. Thus potential misunderstandings are avoided and positive boundaries are clear.

"All the kids are looking forward to your leadership in making their youth group the best ever!" say the parents in the parish to the interim. "I never agreed to run the youth group," the interim responds. "We never even discussed it; it's not what I came here to do!" A very familiar story.

The expectations of the parish leadership are often different than that of the interim pastor. In a well-developed letter of agreement, the issue would have been discussed and a determination made as to the responsibility for leading the youth group and all other related activities. Likewise, the absence of this document can lead to uncertainty, lack of clarity, and confusion.

When interviewing for the position, the prospective interim pastor needs to ask the question, "What am I called to do and be?" Is it to manage the transition process effectively, sensitively, and with great care or is it to be something else? What are the expectations of both parties? Would you be willing to be the adult leader for the youth group or should there be someone else in that role? Conversation must take place and the results of those conversations must be made clear.

It cannot be said enough that all areas of ministry must be thoroughly discussed and decisions made as to where responsibilities lie. The interim pastor, of course, oversees all areas of ministry, but that does not mean that she or he is to be specifically in charge. Because the interim takes on all of the responsibilities of the settled pastor plus the role of coaching the congregation during the transition, adjustments will need to be made. Discussion about what responsibilities the laypeople will take on is important. For example, some interim pastors ask that lay pastors visit the homebound and chronically ill. This is especially appropriate as the interim will barely have time to develop a relationship with these people before he or she moves on. These discussions provide a solid basis for a letter of agreement.

Discussion also needs to take place about the five developmental tasks as described by the Interim Ministry Network (IMN) and in chapter 3 of this book.

While these tasks refer to the work of the congregation, the interim pastor serves as facilitator. Most letters of agreement name the tasks in the preamble, as they are the foundation for ministry during the transition.

The Episcopal Diocese of New York has a template letter of agreement on their website (http://www.dioceseny.org/User_Files/Deployment/E-loa-interim.doc) that is a good example of how the letter of agreement can define the responsibilities of both clergy and lay leaders. Here is their definition of responsibilities:

ROLE AND RESPONSIBILITIES OF INTERIM PASTOR

The Interim Pastor shall lead [name of the church] as pastor, priest and teacher, sharing in the councils of this congregation and of the whole church, in communion with our Bishop. The Interim Pastor represents and extends the ministry which is the Bishop's pastoral and canonical responsibility for congregations in leadership transition. The Interim Pastor shall:

- Work with the Vestry and other lay leaders to maintain the regular schedule of worship services and preaching, pastoral calling on the sick and shut-ins, pastoral offices (weddings, funerals, baptisms) and visiting newcomers.

- Assist with the ongoing administration duties, including the supervision of all parish staff.

- Support the Vestry in its role and responsibilities.

- Work not only in this congregation, but also on behalf of the Diocese, the Church at large, and the community.

- Working closely with the Wardens, Vestry and other parish leaders, with the Bishop and his staff, the major goal of the Interim Pastor's ministry is to prepare the congregation for the coming of the new Rector. To this end, the Interim Pastor shall:

- Help the congregation deal with its grief and any other unresolved issues arising from the Rector's departure.

- Deal with internal conflicts and help heal any divisions within the congregation, working with a Diocesan consultant as appropriate.

- Help Vestry and lay leaders bring about such change as may be needed to align parish life and administration with generally accepted standards in the diocese.

The Interim Pastor shall communicate regularly with the Deployment Officer and the Interim Consultant, but will not work with the Search Committee as they develop the parish profile, position description, solicit and screen candidates. The Interim Pastor is not and will not be a candidate for Rector.

ROLE AND RESPONSIBILITIES OF VESTRY

The Vestry has the responsibility for the church in the absence of a Rector during the interim period. Specific responsibilities include the following:

- Encourage the laity to support and cooperate with the Vestry and the Interim Pastor in pursuit of the tasks and goals of the interim period.

- Responsible for hiring and firing of parish staff during the interim period. While the Vestry should be in consultation with the Interim Pastor regarding any and all personnel matters, the Vestry is ultimately responsible for all staff decisions.

• The Vestry is the legal agent for the congregation in all matters concerning its corporate property and in its relationship with the Interim Pastor.

This agreement reflects the particular expectations held in the Episcopal Diocese of New York regarding the relationship between the interim pastor and the congregation. Other denominations, judicatories, and congregations will have different expectations, which will be defined in their own letters of agreement.

"Is this interim going to change everything?" Of course not. However, change will take place and it will be through the parish's leadership and the interim rector working together. The fact that there is an interim rector and the former rector is no longer present is the most immediate change. Even if the exact same words are used for everything, the personality of the interim will be different. When a new voice speaks old words, there is change. Many subtle things indicate that times have changed. Change is a word that is feared by many and for others is a source of rejoicing.

If there are specific changes to be made, they should be noted very carefully in the letter of agreement. The interim pastor is called to be the best pastor s/he can be and that includes the enabling, facilitating, and leading of a congregation through a most sensitive time. It is not a time of maintenance but rather moving ahead that comes as a result of positive transition and that leads to positive transformation.

What is even more important is to recognize that the interim time is not the same as what we would call the "settled" time, when a more permanent clergy person is in place. The interim is there for specific tasks. Interim ministry is different even though the cleric will be doing many tasks for the ongoing life of the congregation. The congregation sees them in this setting, not the setting of an installed rector.

"We sure wish you could stay as our permanent rector. You have done a great job and we love you!" Most interim pastors hear these words more than once near the end of the interim period. The answer is always, "Thank you, I have an agreement that I honor and therefore I am not a candidate for rector." It is, of course, an unfair advantage if the interim chooses to be a candidate because he or she is in a favorable position by the very fact of his or her presence. Those of us who have chosen interim ministry are never candidates for the position and that should be spelled out clearly in the letter of agreement.

The pastor's discretionary fund is an important subject that is often ignored in letters of agreement. This fund, which is used to help those in special need, has had a history of mismanagement and inappropriate use in many churches. Some judicatories have a policy about this fund during the interim. However, if this is not the case, clearly defined expectations about the use of and accountability for the fund can be helpful in moving a congregation towards transparent financial practices.

Some interims have found that congregations are very sensitive to the amount of time their rector spends "on the job." Church members may make a point of saying, "Oh, I saw your car at church Saturday morning." Everybody quickly figures out which car is the pastor's. For the clergy person who has moved to a new location to serve as interim, there may be a temptation to over-work; after all, family and friends are in another state. This is not healthy for either cleric or congregation. Here is a paragraph from a letter of agreement:

> The interim pastor's scheduled work-week is five days per week, which shall include Sunday activities. The interim pastor is expected to preserve at least one continuous twenty-four-hour period each week solely for personal and family use, and one day per month for quiet/spiritual retreat, both of which may be accumulated quarterly, not interfering with Sunday responsibilities.

This is a fairly standard model of current expectations for the clergy work week. This or something similar should be included in the letter. Other letters describe the work-week in terms of units; one morning or afternoon or evening comprises one unit. Sunday morning counts as two units. Then the work-week can defined as a certain number of units. This format is particularly helpful for the part-time interim pastor.

Many clergy can be timid when it comes to their compensation package. Most think it is only a matter of dollars and cents. They fail to realize that proper negotiation in the spirit of finding a compensation package that is agreeable to all parties is not as difficult as it may seem. Clergy need to know what it is they want and what they actually do need.

One guiding principle is, "Never less than the previous rector." This can be managed in several ways. It may mean the exact same cash dollar amount. Or there could be less cash dollars and more time off instead. This is particularly good when you are some distance from your spouse who will not be living with you because of their own employment. One parish in the middle of the country paid for the airfare for the interim's spouse to visit every five or six weeks from the East Coast. Writing a good contract means that both clergyperson and congregation know their needs, their desires, and what they can do without.

One interim pastor completed a negotiation for the compensation piece of the letter of agreement in a church where the bottom line was the key factor for the parish leadership. The salary was lower than what he had been receiving at his previous interim; however, he agreed to the amount because there were other areas such as the housing equity allowance that would be increased. Health insurance was reimbursed at a higher rate using diocesan guidelines because the interim had a spouse and the previous pastor did not. There are numerous ways to satisfy both parties' monetary concerns.

What about housing? Is there a church-owned house for the interim pastor or is a housing allowance provided? If so, is it adequate for the housing needs of the interim clergy or is the allowance enough to meet the housing costs of the area? Will the whole family be with the interim or will s/he be alone for the most part?

Paying careful attention to all of the financial details benefits both the clergyperson and the congregation. It is common practice for interim clergy who move for an assignment to stay in rented housing. There may not be church-owned housing or the church may use the transition time to remodel the housing. In one such instance, a cleric had signed a year lease for an apartment. The interim's tenure ended abruptly when conflict surfaced and the interim became identified as the problem. This person found herself stuck with several months left to go in a lease but no reason to remain in the town. If the lease had been in the church's name, the cleric could have walked away and the congregation could have used the apartment for the next interim pastor.

As seen in the earlier example from the Episcopal Diocese of New York, most judicatories have a basic letter of agreement form that will be helpful in providing the appropriate boundaries and the standards that need to be met. Judicatory guidelines are an important factor in the negotiations. They can be most helpful in determining salary, housing allowance, health insurance, vacation time, continuing education time, and a fair allowance for same. Some judicatories specify that the interim pastor has limited authority. One colleague reported being in a diocese where the judicatory's letter of agreement template stated that the senior warden was to chair vestry meetings. While this provision had to be included in the contract, the interim pastor and the senior warden agreed that the clergyperson would chair the meetings. Further, both understood that the warden could take back that power at any time.

Another compensation-related item is what is often called "the thirteenth month." A few judicatories include an extra month of compensation at the conclusion of the interim's service. This benefit helps the clergyperson while he or she is in the search process for the next interim position.

Clarity as to the beginning date of the transition ministry and the proposed ending date is necessary if the letter of agreement is to be complete. The easiest, of course, is the start date, as both parties are usually sure when the transition pastor is to begin. However, when the transition time of ministry will end is often not clear to either party. There are numerous factors that will determine the ending date, such as the early arrival of the new rector. The judicatory may have standards for certain situations when a rector leaves after twenty or more years. The congregation will need a longer period for the transition to take place. The period of grief and wonder at what's next will need to be dealt with slowly and deliberately. If there has been a misconduct situation, the congregation will need more time than the average to deal with the issue. Once again there is grief and the question, "How could this happen to us?"

Under what we would call "normal" circumstances, the transition period may be one year to eighteen months, depending on how long the search process takes. The best way to set a beginning and an ending date is to pick the obvious beginning and set the ending as eighteen months later or whatever is appropriate for the situation. In order to allow for flexibility, a statement of change is included stating that either party may terminate the agreement with notification of thirty, sixty, or ninety days. This means that the letter of agreement may be extended or terminated with appropriate notice and prior conversation between the leadership and the clergyperson.

While normally the interim pastor stays until shortly before the settled pastor arrives, there are times to leave early. One colleague reports having been one of three interims on two different occasions. Some situations have a level of complexity that requires the talents of more than one person. In one of the three-interim-cleric situations, the church had a six-year history of being an abusive alcoholic system. The first interim was newly trained but inexperienced in interim ministry. She said that she simply held things together for five months. However, in reality, her stable, self-differentiated, non-anxious presence began the healing process. The second clergyperson had a high level of skill in "after pastor ministry"; however, he left after two-and-a-half years for another position. The third interim pastor was well known for his interim skills in the area. He spent another two years with the congregation. After five years of interim ministry, the congregation had done its work and was ready to call a settled pastor. While this story is unusual, it is good to know that there are always legitimate exceptions to general practice.

The role of the interim in the search process requires careful definition in the letter of agreement. While in most places the interim has absolutely no involvement in the search process, we have seen the interim provide helpful guidance during the process of defining the congregation's profile. As the chapter on strategic planning will show, the interim will work with the people to arrive at a vision for the future. This work can and should show up in the profile document that will serve as a "love letter" to the future rector. However, the interim pastor never has a role in any part of the interview process.

We are aware of at least one case in which an exception to this rule was made. A key staff member was terminated for cause during the last month of the interim. Feelings were high in the congregation about the loss of a beloved staff member. The judicatory official asked the interim pastor to talk with the candidates for the position. He felt it was critical for the new settled rector to have no illusions about the situation. The wardens agreed with the request, so the interim pastor complied.

Regular review of the transitional ministry should take place. Every six months is an appropriate period of time. The review should consider how we are doing? What needs to be done? Are there other ways that we can work together more effectively? These and other questions should be asked so that positive and effective total ministry will take place. Mutual Ministry Review (MMR) is often the tool used for this. Some judicatories' letters of agreement template include a plan for regular MMR. However, if no trained MMR facilitator is available, this process can become a trap. Open and honest evaluation of the shared ministry during the time of transition, with a look at how all the leaders are doing, is much more important than the particular process used.

Finally, it is important that all negotiations take place with people who have the authority to make decisions. This normally would include one or both wardens and the treasurer who have been empowered by the vestry to represent them. The cleric may want to have a consultant with him or her. This insures that all parties concerned are clear in what they are proposing and what they hear. This also prevents one party or the other from dominating or showing unwillingness to truly negotiate.

The letter of agreement should be shared with the vestry in its final form. Copies should be in the hands of all concerned. The entire congregation and the cleric need to be familiar with the content of the letter, as it will set the parameters for their mutual ministry. It is not uncommon for the document to be posted and available to all members of the congregation.

When honest questions have been asked and answered and appropriate financial advice received, the end result will be a clear and fair document to both parties. A well-crafted letter of agreement provides a sound base from which ministry can take place during the time of transition. This document will be the first step toward a new beginning.

Chapter 5

WHY CAN'T THINGS STAY THE SAME?

GEORGE MARTIN

Stagnation in thought or enterprise means death for Christianity as certainly as it does for any other vital movement. Stagnation, not change, is Christianity's most deadly enemy.
— Harry Emerson Fosdick, 1922

One day at church, a friend, whose name was Fred, told me that he had a pretty serious argument with his wife. Fred told me, "You know, that's really rare. Lucille and I hardly ever have a serious argument." "So what caused this particular argument?" I inquired. Fred explained that when he arrived home his wife was standing on the front porch of their house with broom in hand swatting at something above the door. She was knocking down the nest the swallows had started again. Fred told her that maybe they should just let the birds build their nest there, as they had done the previous year when they raised a family of three. His wife pointed out to him what a mess the birds had made of the front porch. Fred said that he came to the defense of the swallows. I asked how the argument had been settled. He told me that the swallows got to stay for another season. And then he said that he had also promised to sweep the porch every day until they left. Fred and Lucille had found a way to work things out and be happy again. The swallows also had a victory.

That story is a metaphor for interim ministry not because there was an argument, or even a threatened divorce, which Fred assured me had never really happened. It is a metaphor because life went on not only for Fred and Lucille, but also for their guests, the swallows. His story was an example of a community (both birds and people) adapting to new possibilities. Of course, it required a little extra on Fred's part, as he had promised to keep the porch clean. A willingness to work a little harder or to try some new things is also characteristic of interim work in a church.

Some churches, when interviewing a prospective interim pastor, often ask the same questions they'd ask when looking for their next permanent pastor. The assumptions are that what every church needs is a great preacher, a sensitive pastor, and an organized administrator. Even though it doesn't hurt if an interim pastor can do these things effectively, what many—if not most—churches need for the interim is a savvy pastor who can help a church look at its real issues.

In Fred's story, his wife Lucille had a practical—some might even say most reasonable—approach to the problem. Just keep destroying the nest and eventually the swallows will disappear. Fred, though, was willing to live with a more complex solution—even one that involved him more personally.

It has been my experience that churches that look for the simple answers to their issues are more like Lucille, simply wanting to return to some state of previous existence. Some families operate with the same kind of assumption when they presume that if they don't talk about problems they will simply go away.

The great danger in any organization, including a church, is complacency—seeking some level of equilibrium in which no one ever rocks the boat. The trouble with this goal is that such an organization is hardly ever able to manage navigating through the tough seas and storms that are certain to come along. The desire for stability or normality is actually harmful and potentially fatal.

Change, of course, is inevitable. Even churches that have had a wonderful period of time with a particular leader will eventually look for another pastor. There will be an end to every pastoral relationship. Every church goes through transition phases William Bridges identifies as the *ending*, the *neutral zone*, and the *beginning*.[1]

The *ending* is the change event that initiates the process of transition. Rarely is the interim pastor involved in the ending of a pastoral relationship, some of which are happily celebrated, and others of which involve acrimony and hurt feelings. The *beginning*, the period following a transition, can be influenced by the leadership of the interim pastor, but this is the phase of church life that is the responsibility of the newly called pastor. The work of the interim occurs during the in-between time or what Bridges calls the *neutral zone*, a time something like the ". . . wilderness through which Moses led his people."² It was a time in the story of the Israelites when something had to die in order for new hope and dreams to be born. Like many such times, there was confusion and it was somewhat disorderly. It was also a very productive, fruitful time that led the people of Israel to see what they called "the promised land." This can be a real gift of interim ministry.

The road maps to follow in an interim period aren't always clear and must nearly always be tailored to fit a particular congregation. While we must always acknowledge the dangers and tensions in the "in-between time," I think we must also embrace the excitement that comes when we consider new possibilities for the future that God has in mind.

Sometimes church leaders think that the task of the interim is to help the congregation experience calm waters or maybe to enter a safe harbor. Often the desire is to find an interim pastor who will just keep things humming along, maintaining a pace and order that is comfortable. There is a term in the biological world which refers to this state. It is *diapause*, defined as a period of physiologically enforced dormancy between periods of activity. We often call it sleep, but that is hardly what most churches need when one pastor leaves and the search is underway for the next leader. Too often, in fact, complacency already has been operative in the life of the church to the point that much of the life and vitality has become dormant. A leadership less inclined toward inertia may be required. A leadership focused on hope, and one that can help a congregation deal with where they have been and where they might be is probably what many churches need when they enter the "in-between time."

A whole series of questions can fruitfully be asked if change is part of the picture of such a time. What if the interim period is to be a time of waking up or a kind of stretching toward new possibilities? What if the interim is the time to ask the hard questions? What if the interim is meant to explore ideas and visions that had been suppressed? What if the interim is the time to try some new things and to allow new leadership to emerge? These are the kinds of questions a "change-oriented" interim pastor will be asking.

Stuckness is the deadly disease of transitional ministry. Everybody knows that there are good habits and there are bad habits. One leads to greater health and vitality, and the other kind are destructive and hurtful. As individuals we are usually mixtures of both kinds of habits with the emphasis, hopefully, being on the habits that make us stronger and more adaptative. Organizations have the same issues. Some habits enhance the life of the community, while other habits endanger it. Often it takes a stranger or a newcomer to recognize what is really happening. It might also require the perspective of Scott Adams, the creator of the "Dilbert" comic strip.

In one comic panel, Dogbert, identified as a career counselor, asks a young man, "What would you like to do with your degree in flower arranging?" The answer given is "I'd like to become a billionaire." Dogbert follows up with another question, "Are you willing to work hard?" The young man replies, "That would sort of defeat the purpose."

A change-oriented interim pastor is sometimes up against the same mentality. Sometimes the congregation is practically somnambulant, having made sure that hardly anything ever changes. Years of calm but safe leadership can effectively, but not productively, keep a lid on nearly every new idea. I once heard an elderly member rejoice in saying, "It's so wonderful. We have all these new members, but they aren't changing a thing." What I knew, and what she hadn't realized, is that things had been changing. In fact, the new members were a consequence of change.

Sometimes an interim pastor can find a congregation that is worn out from a time of great conflict and thinks that all it needs is a time of peace and quiet. I'm reluctant to make sweeping generalizations, but in my experience with interim ministry, many churches enter the interim time having either experienced difficulties marked by division and conflict or by having slowly lost direction and purpose, watching people slowly drift out of sight. Not too surprisingly, the previous pastors started to look for another church that would be easier to lead and perhaps be more personally fulfilling.

The reality of most interim ministry is that an interim pastor enters into a church that is often stuck. Sometimes the war continues. Sometimes the drift continues. Either way it is a dangerous time, unless they have an interim pastor with skills to help the leadership examine the issues that have brought them to this particular critical time.

Peter Koestenbaum is a business consultant who uses his background in philosophy to help define the challenges facing leaders in the world of business. He has said;

> One of the gravest problems in life is self-limitation: We create defense mechanisms to protect us from the anxiety that comes with freedom. We refuse to fulfill our potential. We live only marginally. This was Freud's definition of psychoneurosis: We limit how we live so that we can limit the amount of anxiety that we experience. We end up tranquilizing many of life's functions. We shut down the centers of entrepreneurial and creative thinking; in effect, we halt progress and growth. But no significant decision—personal or organizational—has ever been undertaken without being attended by an existential crisis, or without a commitment to wade through anxiety, uncertainty, and guilt.[4]

Even though he wasn't thinking of a church in a time of transition, Koestenbaum's insights apply to the leadership skills needed of an interim pastor who understands the dynamics of change. In the same interview Koestenbaum paraphrased his favorite philosopher, Soren Kirekegaard:

> Anxiety is the experience of growth itself. In any endeavor, how do you feel when you go from one stage to the next? The answer: You feel anxious. Anxiety that is denied makes us ill; anxiety that is fully confronted and fully lived through converts itself into joy, security, strength, centeredness, and character. The practical formula: Go where the pain is.[5]

The motto "Go where the pain is" might very well be a good sign for an interim pastor to keep on the desk. It is also helpful, though, to know that the pain isn't always obvious. Sometimes it is covered up. Even though I have made it a point to try to understand the pain and anxiety present in a congregation, I am always surprised how difficult it is to discern the truth. After nine months in one congregation, I learned something about some awful things done by a staff person about eight years previously. I asked, "Why did it take so long for me to discover this story?" The response was telling. "We didn't think you would believe us, if we'd told you shortly after you arrived." I only learned about an important part of the past because I had earned their trust, and because I had made it point to keep discovering the truth about the anxiety that was always lying just below the surface. The interim pastor who accepts responsibility for looking at change in a congregation must be willing to ask hard questions and offer a fresh perspective on the real numbers and trends which may have been overlooked or swept under the proverbial rug. Willingness to engage in this kind of work is key for both congregation and the interim pastor.

In some ways it is actually easier to be an interim in the midst of a conflicted church because there is a high likelihood that some people felt quite neglected or excluded. Once people take sides in a church conflict, it seems inevitable that some will side with their pastor, and others will distance themselves, feeling that they can no longer trust their pastor. An interim pastor will initially hear both sides of such stories as a few people seek to discover if this is someone who can be trusted. This means that an interim pastor may find it easy to discover some of the war stories. Even if these stories aren't readily shared, the prudent intentional interim will make every effort to seek out the truth of what happened. It is critical to listen to a great many people, being careful not to take sides. The interim pastor who addresses the causes of conflict and who creates bridges between different warring parts of a congregation is offering a great gift to the pastor about to be called.

The task of the creative interim pastor in such a situation is to create bridges, especially to those who've been disinherited or who haven't had their voice heard. It is good to be suspicious of those who are most vocal and who continue to wield their verbal weapons. The neutrality that the interim pastor can bring to a particular issue, though, is the gift that is needed, allowing some to express their true feelings.

A term that applies to this kind of leadership is *interpathy*. It is described as

> that depth of relationship when an outsider to a particular host community develops a burden in her heart for that community.

It refers to the capacity for an outsider to pick up a community's sense of values, what has hurt them, and where they're headed as a people group. It is a form of identification so deep that the guest/missionary has almost become one of the host tribe.[6]

Connected to interpathy is the fundamental requirement that the interim pastor is something like a cultural anthropologist discovering what Kotter calls the "corporate culture." In an example from his book *Leading Change*, directed at business leaders, John Kotter notes than much of the subtle resistance to new ideas comes from the often repeated, and therefore constantly reinforced message, "Yes, but, blah-blah blah-blah, technology, blah-blah blah-blah."[7] In the church the message often is, "We tried that once and it didn't work."

It is highly unlikely that an interim pastor will actually change the culture within the church because this is the ultimate challenge —allowing an organization to overcome resistance to change. In Kotter's analysis, eight things are needed to be an effective change leader in the business world. The last task, indeed the hardest one, is changing norms and values than generally guide people who belong to a particular organization. In his words,

Culture is not something that you manipulate easily. . . . Culture changes only after you have successfully altered people's actions, after the new behavior produces some group benefit for a period of time and after people see the connection between the new actions and the performance improvement.[8]

The interim pastor intent on helping a congregation discover new opportunities for life and ministry doesn't have the luxury of time. Nevertheless, he or she can discover those positive norms and values still operative in the church community—or at least those that were present in the past, perhaps in the so-called "glory days" as many church people think about the past. Most likely those days of "blessed memory" were marked by a sense of urgency, meaning that people were trying to maximize the opportunity that demanded their very best. It is rather ironic that many churches, having fallen into a kind of malaise, remember their best days as filled will growth, energy, and challenges. Those stories, if properly filtered, translated, and interpreted by a wise interim, may help lay the foundation for a new vision, and maybe even a recovery of that same spirit that guided the church in the past.

It has been my experience that the discovery of the values that once permitted growth and adaptation is not only like discovering gold, but it makes the whole interim enterprise the exciting and fulfilling ministry it is meant to be. This part of the interim process is what I find personally transforming, as it moves me out my research mode into pastoral leadership with a sense of mission even for the short term. Hirsch and Frost have it right. You almost become one of them. I think I captured the essence of this in one interim when I was able to tell the congregation one Sunday, after being there about three months, "We have to be honest. This church has some serious issues and problems. What you need to know though is that I love your problems. And as people, you're good people. We can address these problems together."

I know of a church where there was great conflict still brewing about the design of the new church. A terrible fire had destroyed their hundred-year-old church and its parish hall and educational wing. The embers from the fire had hardly cooled when people started to take sides over the design of the new church. Would it be built just like their old church or would it represent the insights of the liturgical movement that led to a new prayer book that was being used? Those wanting their old church back were outvoted when the congregation chose to design their church more in a contemporary Gothic style, but the opposition never quite gave up the battle, using their most powerful weapon—their wealth. A year and a half into the construction of the new church, those wanting their old wooden church back were still withholding money. They had not supported the capital fund-raising effort needed to complete the new church building.

The interim pastor arrived in the second year of the construction process. It would be two more years before the church would be completed, but the question was how it could be finished if they didn't have enough money. The church sought the services of a fund-raising consultant who gave his report just as the interim pastor arrived. His conclusion was that there was no way that the church could raise the money needed. Twelve months later, though, the church had raised $2.5 million, and the construction project was back on track. More importantly, many of those new pledges were coming from people who had been reluctant to give in the first place. Even more significantly, one of the most distinguished members of the church, known for her opposition to the approved design, was one of the first to go on a tour of the partially completed church, as soon as that was possible.

What changed? Bridges were built. The truth was given and received. There was recognition that some people had done and said things that were hurtful.

Some naming of the negative aspects of recent history always needs to be articulated. At the same time there are often core values in the church which may have been dormant but are positive and need to be articulated. In the church described above, which completed a successful and necessary capital funds drive, the forgotten values included pride and responsibility, a love of hospitality, and openness to all kinds of people. Emphasizing these values not only shed new light on their past but also opened some doors to the future. The interim made it a point to emphasize the need for forgiveness and reconciliation. The entire process generated hope for the church and planted the seeds for the work of the new settled pastor. They called a mission-oriented pastor who helped them properly dedicate their new church facility.

While it was possible in that particular church to reignite a stalled capital fund-raising effort during the interim time, this isn't always the case. An interim pastor should never make assumptions about what can and can't happen. In one situation the interim task as it was discerned within the first few months was to help the leadership realize that they shouldn't proceed with the plans that were underway for raising money to pay off debt incurred when an adjacent piece of property had been purchased. The telling sign was that the approval passed by a single vote. Almost a third of the congregation was opposed to the purchase. The interim discovered that the decision had been made in haste and people had hardly been given a chance to share their ideas. It was another situation in which some significant people had been marginalized.

The interim period can be a time for new leadership to be cultivated. I have already named "stuckness" as one of the diseases an interim pastor will likely find in a congregation. This concept often applies to the leadership of the parish. In many churches one of the easiest, but most dangerous, patterns is the habit of relying on a narrow-based, sometimes ever decreasing, coterie of leaders for making decisions. Often these are people with demonstrated history in the congregation and visible long-standing commitments to the church. In the more enmeshed churches, it is almost a standing rule that it takes time, often a long time, to be accepted as a leader. It has been my experience that some clergy also settle into a leadership style of trusting a smaller group of leaders because it is simply the easier way to make decisions, even if they are unwilling to embrace vision and courage on behalf of the future.

An interim pastor needs to ask questions about how decisions were made in order to assess the viability and strength of a congregation. Insights from the world of evolutionary biology are helpful here. Organisms that adapt themselves and are able to respond to immediate threats are those that usually survive. The force of life is at work in all of nature as well as in the life of the church. As the journalist Natalie Angier has written:

> If much of nature looks designed, that's because it is designed. Not from the outside in, but from the inside throughout, on the fly, by life striving to fulfill the prophecy of itself, and to remain, at all costs and by any pathway or laugh track, here on Earth, among itself, alive.[9]

While adaptation marks success in the biological world, many interim clergy often find themselves in churches that have stopped evolving or adapting. One of the questions I have learned to ask is, "Which committees or structures no longer exist?" A parallel question concerns events or programs that have disappeared.

An important question for the interim pastor to pose comes from Alan Hirsch, who asks people who are in stuck churches, "If you could start over again from scratch, would you do it in the same way?" Hirsch reports that the usual answer is "No." He follows up with the question, "Then why are you not changing now?"[10]

In terms of leadership, the interim pastor is probably freer to create some listening groups and to form some new committees if such might be helpful to the work of the church. I discovered in one church, for example, a real lack of social events in which people came together to experience community. After about four months of making friends, I called four women together who had an interest in helping people experience fellowship. They made an amazing discovery at their first meeting. They were all "only children," which they understood as a kind of giftedness for getting things done. It wasn't long before the church began to experience a variety of social events that started to help everyone make new friends and feel more connected to the church.

A more complex set of challenges awaits the interim pastor looking at worship issues. I can't remember where I heard the story about the bishop who witnessed liturgical dance at a particular parish. In the middle of worship a young woman appeared at the back and came dancing and cavorting (liturgically) up the aisle. She laid a lily at the feet of the bishop. The bishop whispered to the pastor, "If she asks for your head on a platter, she can have it."

That story serves as a kind of warning. Liturgical innovations can stir up deep emotions. It is not unusual to hear clergy tell stories about someone threatening to leave the church or withhold their pledge if some aspect of worship is changed. It may be safer to walk across some battle-worn minefields than to think about making changes in some worship services. Mindful of the dangers inherent in changing worship, I nonetheless maintain that this is an area for interim pastors to give serious consideration. Congregations that have lost their sense of mission and purpose will often be marked by worship that is boring or uninspiring.

I have served churches marked by a variety of worship-related issues. One may have suffered through years of dull sermons. In another church the choir complained about singing the same thirty to forty hymns all the time. Another church told me stories about the way the pastor yelled at people who made mistakes in worship. Some churches have worship guides that are practically useless. Others have worship that at times is plainly weird and not true to the church's historical or denominational roots.

Rather than try to address all the worship issues latent in the congregation, however, a savvy interim is best advised to suggest changes that are subtle and less likely to create controversy. If the congregation becomes more flexible and open, that is far more important to its future than any particular new addition to its worship or program. I have found, for example, that simply adding a word of welcome to the worship lends a more personal invitation that is often lacking. Too often the pastoral dimension of worship is lost over time, and yet people often come to a church not only to encounter God, but to discover real community.

It is also well known that even many small congregations can be unintentionally cold to a first-time guest, even though the image maintained in the congregational story is that it is a most friendly congregation. The interim pastor is in a unique position, at least for the first month or two, to make an accurate assessment about the congregation's real level of friendliness. I have found that one test of this value is to ask people to wear nametags, not simply for my benefit, but as a mark of the way we should always be ready to welcome guests into the community. I was particularly struck by the willingness of one rather small congregation to wear their nametags. I had wrongly assumed at the outset that there would be great resistance to this practice. Making premature assumptions is a danger that most interim clergy need to learn to avoid.

Even if there are some aspects of worship that are abysmal, my sense is that the wise course for leadership is to only make changes within a more collaborative framework. Quite frequently, even though everyone has opinions about worship, very few have ever been actively engaged in the planning of worship. Even if there is a worship committee, that group may have been restricted to dealing with superficial aspects of planning. An interim period can have a missing educational component. In the case of worship, for example, people can expand their understanding of liturgy. Decisions can be made based on answers to the "why" questions, as in "Why are we having a extra service on Christmas Eve focused on families with very young children?" If the answer is rooted in some of the core values and connected to the church's sense of mission rather than based on someone's personal preference, there is a high likelihood that a great many will be supportive of that particular change.

There's a line from an old hymn that speaks the truth of this fact: "New occasions teach new duties."[11] There is a kind of freedom that the interim pastor has to say, "Why don't we just try this? After all, this is an interim time, and we're not exactly setting anything in place for the long haul." If a new addition to worship is successful as measured by increased attendance or by favorable reviews from a number of people, chances are, of course, that there will be a desire to see it repeated. That's not all bad.

The last time I began interim ministry in a church I showed the congregation on my first Sunday a small poster that I promised would be kept on my desk through the interim. The poster shows a childlike drawing of a catlike animal with a figure perched on the saddle, ready to jump, as it were. The poster says, "I'm a good jumper," he said, but I'm not so good at landing. Maybe you should stay closer to the ground then, I said. And he shook his head and said the ground was the whole problem in the first place."[12]

At the end of that interim pastorate, a number of people thanked me for the various kinds of events we had, for the changes we'd made, and for the good times we had together. A few of them remembered the poster and thought I had taught them how to jump. That may be what some congregations need, but this one needed to change its perspective "on the ground." I think we moved the ground. As a consequence of trying some new things and looking at their issues in a fresh way, they were no longer so afraid of falling or failing. The ground had somehow shifted. A sense of adventure and excitement had entered the back door of this church and there was a buzz waiting for the new pastor as people started to wonder what God had in mind for them. We might say this congregation experienced change in the interim, but in reality it was simply a period of setting the stage for a whole new time of missionary energy and excitement.

It is true that the interim pastor is present for but a short period of time, but that can be a time of great meaning and importance in the life of a congregation, especially if that community starts to become more awake to the possibilities of mission and service. Perspectives can change in a congregation if some issues are faced, if reconciliation occurs, and if there is a resolve to live with a deeper sense of purpose and focus. All of this can be the door that opens the church for a whole new chapter of witness and ministry. The interim pastor who brings a sense of urgency to the transition period and who couples that with hope is offering a real gift to the congregation and its next pastor. It is enough if the interim pastor looks back in a few years and sees a congregation that is thriving, growing, and changing with the times for the purpose of serving God and all God's people.

Notes

1. William Bridges, *Managing Transitions: Making the Most of Change* (Reading MA: Perseus Books, 1991).

2. Ibid., 37.

3. Gerald Locklin, "where we are," in *Good Poems*, ed. Garrison Keillor (New York: Penguin Books, 2002), 286.

4. Peter Koestenbaum, as quoted in an interview by Polly Labarre, "Do you have the will to lead?" *Fast Company*, March 2000, 222–230.

5. Ibid.

6. Michael Frost and Alan Hirsch, *The Shaping of Things to Come* (Peabody, MA: Hendricksen Publishers, 2003), 64.

7. John P. Kotter, *Leading Change* (Boston, MA: Harvard Business School Press, 1996), 147.

8. Ibid., 156.

9. Natalie Angier, *The Canon: A Whirligig Tour of the Beautiful Basics of Science* (Boston: Houghton Mifflin Co., 2007), 172.

10. Frost and Hirsch, *Shaping of Things to Come*, 62.

11. James Lowell, "Once to every man and nation," 1845.

12. This poster is called "Good Jumper" by artist Brian Andreas. Available through The Story People (http://www.storypeople.com).

Chapter 6

WHY WE FIGHT

TERRY FOLAND

Conflict is not an unusual phenomenon in churches. The earliest church communities had conflicts. The writer of the Gospel of Matthew has Jesus giving a four-step plan for how to deal with someone who "sins against you" (Matthew 18:15–20). Those steps are clear and concise and indicate that the early church was having serious conflicts. I will discuss those specific steps and what Jesus seemed to be teaching later in this chapter.

Conflicts in churches today are experienced more often than they have been in the past and seem to have more devastating consequences than they did in past centuries. This chapter will explore some of the reasons why conflict is prevalent in churches today and why the current church culture in the Western world (in the United States and Canada especially) is so vulnerable to personal likes and dislikes that lead to serious divisions and conflicts.

Conflict is often exacerbated during an interim ministry time. On the one hand, members can be anxious about the future and they react with more emotion than they might at other times. Leaders, as well as other members, may wonder why the pastor left and may be looking for someone on which to place the blame. The stage is set for conflict, especially if there was controversy around the dissolution of the clergy—congregation partnership. On the other hand, the interim period is an excellent time to address conflict. Interim pastors are more able to confront and do truth-telling since they are there with a specific purpose of helping the church through the transition agenda, of which conflict is often the dominant issue. Interim ministry specialists have received specialized training to help them be conflict managers and often have a personality that does not avoid conflict. Very often the contracting process for an interim ministry will surface the need for addressing the conflict situations in the congregation.

Church members fight about all kinds of issues. I have discussed several of those prevalent issues in a chapter entitled "Understanding Conflict and Power" in the book *Temporary Shepherds: A Congregational Handbook for Interim Ministry*.[1] Those issues include church identity; who is in charge or control; what we believe; how we worship; role expectations of leaders, especially of clergy; limited resources; focus of mission and ministries; perceived or real malfeasance or misconduct of ministers. This chapter is about why church members fight with each other more than it is about what the issues are over which they fight.

Conflict may be defined in several different ways. For the purpose of this chapter, I define conflict as any interaction that causes the "actors" to feel angry, hurt, disillusioned, disturbed, or disappointed with the other "actor" or "actors" of a given transaction. Conflict may be positive or negative. It may lead the persons involved to clarify their positions on a given issue, for example, and that is usually a positive thing. Or it may cause persons to withdraw and become alienated from each other and that is a negative thing. The real issue is not the presence of conflict, but how the principle actors in a conflict react and especially how they treat each other. Even in the most serious disagreements, the principles should treat each other with respect and dignity. The key is to focus on the issues and not on the individuals as the object of the conflict.

So why do we fight? I have identified nine primary reasons that I have observed in church conflicts I have worked with as a church consultant with the Alban Institute and as a church executive with my denomination, The Christian Church (Disciples of Christ). I will define the factors and illustrate each one with examples from real church situations. I will not identify the specific churches or persons due to respect for them and their right to privacy.

1. The deeply engrained consumer attitude.

I think the recent television advertisement for a well-known credit card company defines the attitude I have repeatedly observed in church members who are engaged in church fights. The message of the ad is stated powerfully by the voice-over singing repeatedly, "I want it all, I want it all, and I want it now!" The message intended seems clearly to be one that says you can get it now by charging it, whatever the "it" is, and never have to be accountable for paying the price. Max out the card and you can always get another one. "All" is never defined, I suppose so that the targeted consumers are free to let that be whatever really excites or pleases them. This is really a form of instant gratification and goes counter to the so-called Protestant work ethic of deferred gratification. Deferred gratification was a concept that was prevalent prior to the last half of the twentieth century and meant, in effect, that if you wanted something you saved the money until you could pay for it and then you purchased it.

This attitude is one that causes church members to expect that the church will provide me what I personally want immediately or I will get angry with the church leaders and blame them for not providing whatever that is. For example, many church members today expect worship to be entertaining and want the minister and the worship leaders to provide a worship experience every Sunday that is as good as their favorite TV program. When that is not provided, they blame the minister and the lay worship leaders.

One church fight I "refereed" was largely about budget priorities. The major issue was on how much money should be spent for outreach causes that helped persons who were not church members over against how much money should be spent on what church members felt they wanted and needed for themselves. The underlying motivation was the consumer attitude of getting what I want when I want it.

2. The dominating competitive culture.

Winning is everything. We are taught that from our early years in sports and in games of all kinds. We are conditioned to want to win. Competition is not wrong in itself, but when winning is the top priority, the church loses. That attitude carries over into our church activities. We are prone to choosing sides when there is a conflict. And the win-at-all-costs determines how we carry on our interactions instead of regarding the issues objectively.

"Whose idea was that?" often becomes more important to find

out than exploring what the idea is about and what it may offer for the church as a community. The team attitude leads to packing boards and committees with all the right people. The right people will vote for our side. It is a sign of an unhealthy church when the motivating factor for decisions is "who wants it" instead of "what is the idea and how will it help us do our ministries and mission?"

One church I consulted with had this down to a "game" which all the members had come to accept. Side A would get angry or displeased with the pastor and get the board packed with enough votes to fire the pastor. They would then control the search process for the next pastor and call someone who would agree with them on the important issues. Of course, the opposition—Side B—would begin to look for faults of the new pastor and begin working on getting church members to be critical with accusations and surprise attacks on the pastor and the lay leadership in board meetings. Within about two years, the pastor would either just give up and resign, or Side B would get enough votes in the board to fire this pastor. Then the cycle would begin again.

Each time the cycle was played out, some members of the church would get disgusted and leave. But the goal of winning was so strong that the core leaders of the two main church factions either could not or would not change their tactics for the good of the whole church. The competitive attitude was more important than anything else. After listening to about fifty percent of the congregation, I was ready to begin my report to the church board. The denial was over-whelming. When I reminded them that in about twenty-two years the church had changed pastors five times and that there was clear evidence that the leadership had shifted each time the pastor was forced out, one member present said with resounding conviction, "I guess we have just had a series of getting bad pastors!"

3. Payback or revenge for previous actions.

This factor is similar and often the result of the previous factor. The script runs something like this: "You got our pastor out; now we are going to get your pastor out." Of course the "game" is played with a lot of subtlety and overt denial. Hardly any church leader is going to openly admit they are seeking revenge. The issue is usually couched in terms of what the current pastor has done wrong this time.

One of the defining factors for payback or revenge is finding fault. It is my experience that the principle players in this reciprocal process are genuinely unaware of what they are doing. In that same church where one key leader indicated she believed they had received a series of bad pastors, the following conversation took place. Question from me as consultant: "What are the common factors that were present in the problems that caused the previous pastors to be dismissed or fired?" One answer from one of the church leaders: "They all failed to understand who was really in charge here." A second answer from another lay leader: "There was no common mistake; they each made a different set of poor decisions or judgments." My analysis of why each pastor had been asked to resign or was voted out by the board also indicated that the presenting issues over which the dissolution of the relationship as pastor and congregation was instituted were different in each of the five separations.

When the major motivating factor is payback or revenge, the issue is not the real reason for the action of firing the pastor. Actually, almost any issue will do. The real reason is the payback factor itself. In another church, it became quite clear that the group that was hounding the most recent pastor had been the main group of supporters of the previous pastor. It simply was not heard or at least not comprehended by that group of leaders. The group wanting revenge will always put the focus on the presenting current problem or issues and be unwilling even to consider the larger pattern of what the repeating dynamic really indicates. We fight in churches because we let the motivation of getting even overrule our sense of fairness and objectivity.

4. Pastor-centered churches.

A pastor-centered church is one in which the major focus is on the pastor who can deliver excellent sermons and is a dynamic and charismatic leader. People will come from miles around to hear the sermons. Membership will usually grow rapidly as satisfied attendees spread the word of an experience of worship (or at least a good and enter-taining sermon) which they want to share with others. "Come hear our preacher; you will be amazed and entertained." The minister takes on an aura of legendary proportions. And it is great as long as it lasts. But often the great speaker moves on to even greener pastures and a larger venue and the church is left with a pleasant memory and a never-ending hangover. No pastor can ever seem to match the great orator of the past. Every pastor who follows is compared to the "great one," and they never can live up to that glorious reputation. And so we fight in this church situation because we secretly want to blame the present pastor for our loss of members and rapid and continuing decline. The real reason for the decline is that the reason for many members to attend worship—the great preacher—is now gone, so they have no reason to continue to attend.

Other notable characteristics of clergy-centered churches that are nearly always present include:

- The pastor is always the one who sets the goals and provides the inspiration for the church's mission and ministries.

- The pastor is viewed as being "my chaplain" and is ex-pected to be available when "I" am in need. The chaplain is the rescuer when "I" am in trouble.

- There is a dominant sense of parent—child relations with the pastor as parent and the members as children. Dependency is the operative mode.

- There is a reluctance to disagree openly with the pastor because s/he is a hero and you are not supposed to chal-lenge heroes in public.

- The pastor may exhibit behaviors that normally would not be acceptable in personal relations, but is not confronted by church members, due to the exalted status granted to the pastor.

A pastor-centered church will usually fail to engage in other meaningful ways those members who only come to hear the preacher. These members, who are there because of the great preaching, will usually fall away after the great preacher leaves. And many who remain active will continue to "worship" the legendary hero from a distance. They often will find reasons to go and visit the previous pastor in the distant city and come back with glowing stories of how things are growing rapidly there just as they did here. They will make remarks about the previous pastor without regard to what those remarks may do to belittle the current pastor, who is struggling to do ministry of many kinds as well as preach the sermon every Sunday.

And so we fight. We fight about what the present minister is doing that is wrong. We blame the minister for the decline when the real fault is with those who have stopped attending because their reason for attending is now gone. One pastor of such a situation reported that well-meaning members would come into his office and say something like, "I wasn't sure I should talk with you about this, but I called the previous pastor (and would name him) and he said it would be all right to bring it up with you." And the well-meaning members would never realize what that communicated. The message the current pastor got was something like, "You don't really measure up to the standards of the previous pastor. I still go to him for advice and counsel." Or the message was, "You had better agree with what the previous pastor said about this subject or situation." The pastor reporting this story indicated that he believed the members who did this had not a clue that they were hurting him and that they genuinely did not know what a negative effect this behavior had on him.

Clergy-centered churches are extremely vulnerable to clergy misconduct—sexual misbehavior, mismanagement of church finances, or abuse of power. Interim ministers who follow clergy misconduct, or where misconduct was perceived even if never substantiated, often report the tendency to blame the next pastor for everything that goes wrong. Such clergy are called "after pastors" in the materials written about churches and clergy misconduct. The after pastors also report that they feel a great deal more stress than is normal in most churches and that they are "lightning rods" for anything that is open for disagreement or conflict among the church leaders.

In one church where I was consulting, the worship department was being pressured to make some major changes in the service of worship prior to the interim pastor being called. The changes were instituted and after a period of six months the feedback was so strong that the worship department reversed the changes and went back to the previous order of the service of worship. When the worship department chairperson reported the action to reverse the decision, she did so only after indicating that it was the interim pastor who wanted the changes in the first place. "No one," the interim pastor reported, "challenged that statement even though it was clear that [he] was not even in the church employment at the time the decision was made."

5. The urge to control.

Almost everyone wants to control things with which they are involved. Control is essential for keeping meetings from erupting into chaos or evolving into a state of *laissez–faire* or even complete disarray with nothing being accomplished. The problem comes when one party or another has such high control needs that they believe they must control everything in which they are involved. At the deepest level, control exerts itself because the person who is controlling believes s/he is the only one who can make things go right. Such an individual generally has a clear concept or idea of what should be the outcome of a given situation or issue and they must see to it that this happens. When control needs are strong, the person will often not hesitate to manipulate things so they will go as they want them to go. Manipulation will lead to distortions and misrepresentation of facts. The person who must control will often also not be averse to lying to make a strong case for his or her position. And s/he may even go to great extremes of convincing other persons to be allies in getting what s/he wants.

Control may be managed by how an agenda is put together for a crucial meeting. Control may be managed by either misstating an item or by framing the issue in such a way as to highlight its negative aspects instead of the positive elements. In one church, the moderator of the board often manipulated the agenda by adding items after the executive committee had agreed to the agenda for that meeting. Her tactic of surprise would leave those who were on the opposite side unprepared to discuss the item adequately. She also would present as though fact the opinion of an authority, such as an attorney or a judicatory official, when she had not really even consulted them. If challenged by anyone, she was quick to play the victim and appeal to others to back her up. Finally, though, the board as a whole refused to back her up on some important issues. She then played the victim even more and resigned from her position as board chair along with several others whom she had convinced that her position was justified. The board as whole, however, did not fall for that tactic and let her and the others go without verbal protest. In this instance, the board matured and realized how her control needs had caused much stress in the meetings and they moved on without regret or guilt feelings.

6. Stress makes people do crazy things.

When individuals are under stress, they often revert to childish behaviors or they react out of previous transactions where they have been hurt. For example, a man or woman who has been mistreated by a spouse or parent may strongly identify the pastor or lay leader with whom s/he is in conflict with the abuser from the past. Most of those who do this usually do not even realize what they are doing. The behavior will seem appropriate to the perpetrator because there has been transference of emotion so strong that the identity of the perceived opposition is totally real for the one who is stressed out this much. Childish behaviors include such things as wanting to choose up sides, pouting, playing the victim, distorting information to fit one's own purposes, and outright lying to make the opponent look bad.

7. Lack of stewardship foundation.

Churches that do not have a good stewardship foundation are more apt to be churches with repeated conflict patterns. Giving financial support that is a tithe or percent of a family income seems to foster an attitude that makes conflict less prevalent. When there is conflict, there is a more open attitude regarding the way people treat each other. My observation is that people who make serious financial commitments to their church are people who are generous in other dimensions of their lives also. So when a conflict arises, these persons are willing to commit to working the issues through to some satisfactory conclusion.

The opposite observation is that persons who do not give generously of their financial resources are more apt to fight about all sorts of things in the church and especially financial issues. One congregation had a large endowment and a farm the church had inherited from a previous wealthy member. The income from the two sources was sufficient to underwrite about sixty-five percent of the church operating budget. Members over the years had established a pattern of only giving enough to support the other thirty-five percent of the budget and that became their stewardship program. Instead of using the inherited income for mission and outreach, they used it as an excuse to give less from their own resources. There was an attitude of miserliness developing in this church. Anyone who wanted to change the way in which the "windfall" was to be used was accused of meddling with a good thing for all the church members. When the interim minister insisted that the board members hear the will read again—the source of the endowment fund principle and the farm income—several members stridently objected. The interim pastor insisted, however, and the will was read again. It was clear that the will indicated that the income was to be used by the church for mission and outreach only. Several of the members argued that the money supporting the operating budget was "outreach" because "we are out in the community every day and that is outreach." One member said, "We can justify using the $65,000 we spent on repairing the roof of the fellowship hall because we have community groups who use our building sometimes." (Never mind that the only group currently using the building was a group that had a once-a-year dinner event in the fellowship hall, and they paid the church a rental fee when they did.) And so the fight continued in that church for several more years about how the money could be used and about how to interpret the phrase in the will that said the "income could only be used for mission and outreach purposes."

8. It is all about me.

Church fights are also often centered on the attitude of selfishness. What does the church provide for me and my family? It is all about me, instead of what I can do to help carry out the mission of my faith community. Disgruntled members will often say things like, "The worship just does not do anything for me any more." Or, "I don't like the way the minister uses resource materials that are not biblical enough. I just want the gospel preached." When worship becomes the object of what pleases the membership instead of the focus being on how we best worship God, then there is a ripeness in that church for church conflicts. Of course, members should be satisfied with the worship experiences. It is when the emphasis gets out of place and the personal needs become the primary motivator above the main purpose of worship, which is to glorify God and to inspire people to Christian action, that problems arise.

"It is all about me" may also include fighting about the schedule on Sunday morning. Personal habits, such as meeting friends for Sunday lunch at a popular local restaurant, may be the driving force behind the argument to have worship early on Sunday morning. But other members may want to sleep late on Sunday, so they argue for a later time. Even having two or more services on a weekend may not alleviate the conflict since some will prefer the early time for the service they like and vice versa.

9. Genuine differences and opinions.

We also fight about genuine differences and opinions. I define genuine conflict as being conflict over which there are two or more equally legitimate positions or conclusions that can be reached on a given issue or concern. Church members can have legitimate differences on such things as values, preferences for how something should be done, opinions about what church priorities should be, and on various theological premises. For example, some members may be biblical literalists and others may tend to believe in the Bible as being largely stories of allegory or myth that can be interpreted in different ways. These are both legitimate perspectives and neither party is apt to be able to convince the opposition that they are right and the other person is wrong. So they can learn to live together and learn to reap the richness of what each perspective can bring to lively discussions of the weekly Bible lessons.

Many churches today find it is necessary to provide more than one type of service of worship in order to meet the varying preferences of how people worship. People have personal differences about what they like in church music. Some prefer the "old gospel hymns"; others like the hymns that were written during the Protestant Reformation; still others may prefer the music that is emerging today from the so-called contemporary songwriters. The problem is when one only person or group exerts their power and influence and demands that things be the way they want them, because, after all, their view or taste or preference is the "right one." Then conflicts emerge.

Healthy congregations fight well.

Conflict in churches and elsewhere is more about relationships than it is about resolving a given problem or issue. In healthy congregations, there may be open disagreement but there is always respect for the opposing parties. In healthy congregations, opposing individuals or groups stay in communication and conversation with each other until they reach some satisfactory conclusion that everyone can live with, even if some may not be totally in agreement with the resolution. Healthy congregations create open processes in which the necessary dialogue can take place. Healthy congregations regularly put into practice the spiritual disciplines of prayer, Bible study, and honest dialogue when they are facing critical decisions that can threaten the well-being of the congregation.

One model that is often followed is the one described in the Gospel of Matthew (18:15–17), which can outlined in four steps. When there is a problem between members of the church, they should:

1. Go directly to the other person and discuss the problem.

2. If the problem persists, the one seeking resolution should take another person or two with him or her and try again.

3. If that still does not get resolution, then the problem should be brought before a responsible church body (pastoral relations committee or other appropriate group or the official church board).

4. If that does not get resolution, then just let it go.

Matthew also has this model followed with a passage (18:21–22) that indicates the principle of forgiveness needs to be offered as often as forgiveness is necessary. The formula of seventy times seven really means we don't keep track of the number of times we offer forgiveness. We offer it as often as it is needed.

So we fight because we can. We fight because we are conditioned by many cultural practices and history. We can choose to fight well and fair and grow as a result. Or we can choose to fight with a win-at-all-costs attitude and eventually discover that all really lose as a result. Transitions or interims can be those times when a congregation is intentional about how it deals with conflict and perhaps be the time when resolve is made to "do conflict better" in the future.

Note

1. Roger S. Nicholson, ed., *Temporary Shepherds: A Congregational Handbook for Interim Ministry* (Herndon, VA: Alban Institute, 1998).

Chapter 7

WHAT IS THE APPRECIATIVE INQUIRY APPROACH TO TRANSITION?

Rob Voyle

Since its beginnings in the mid-1980s, appreciative inquiry[1] has become a preferred method of whole-system interventions in the organizational development world. It has been successfully used in both large and small corporate and not-for-profit organizations including church and para-church organizations. The word "appreciate" means to recognize and value the worth of something, to express gratitude for something of value, or to grow in value. To inquire means to explore or to ask questions of something. When put together in the process known as "appreciative inquiry," all these meanings are operative. People are invited to explore what is valuable in their organizations and the very act of inquiry causes what is valuable to grow.

Appreciative inquiry may be viewed in two different ways. One simple approach is to view it as a positive organizational development tool that uses a "5D" method of define, discover, dream, design, and deliver[2] process to facilitate strategic planning or respond to organizational needs. This approach is best known for its use of community-wide interviewing into best experiences of the organization. However, this simplistic view of appreciative inquiry will result in a process that offers minimal assistance in many transitional ministry settings.

An alternative approach is to see appreciative inquiry as a way of being and acting in the world in a life-giving manner. This perspective seeks to discover and grow the life-giving core of an organization rather than simply work to reduce the presence and impact of problems. David Cooperrider, the founder of appreciative inquiry, describes it this way:

Appreciative inquiry is based on a reverence for life. . . .
It is an inquiry process that tries to apprehend the factors
that give life to a living system and seeks to articulate those
possibilities that can lead to a better future. More than a
method or a technique, the appreciative mode of inquiry is a
means of living with, being with, and directly participating
in the life of human systems in a way that compels one to inquire into the deeper life-generating essentials and potentials
of organizational existence.[3]

In my work helping congregations in transition, I have integrated the appreciative inquiry perspective with the resource-based
strategies of psychiatrist Milton Erickson[4] and his students, together
with contemplative spirituality as found in the mystical traditions of
Christianity and Buddhism in order to create the appreciative way.[5]
This lifts appreciative inquiry out of the realm of simply being a
positive strategic development tool to an incarnational way of being
and living in the world that offers a transformational perspective
and approach to any individual or organization's life experience. It is
from this appreciative way perspective that I will address managing
transitions.

While positive in its orientation, this appreciative approach goes
beyond simply being positive to focusing on and then growing that
which is life-giving. Positive and negative are judgments that depend
on a person's value system. Some may consider something positive
while others might consider it negative. To transcend the possibility
of positive—negative judgments and arguments, appreciative inquiry
identifies and focuses on the life-giving realities in the congregation
rather than simply focusing on what is considered positive. Once
these life-giving realities have been discovered, the congregation is
invited to wonder corporately what would happen if they were to
focus on and grow these qualities. This corporate focus on growing
what is life-giving protects against a näive optimism that unrealisti-
cally hopes things will get better without developing strategies to
ensure that positive change will actually take place.

This focus of appreciative inquiry radically contrasts many organizational development approaches based on the medical model that

assess, diagnose, and treat problems. These pathology or problem-reduction approaches are based on the assumption that organizational development occurs through the elimination of problems or threats to the organization's life.

However, difficulties often arise when these approaches are used with organizations because diagnosis is essentially a sophisticated form of judgment and blame. While diagnosis may be helpful in the medical context of treating physical ailments, its use with human organizations often results in defensiveness, judgment, and blame with increasing levels of alienation. This leads to organizational problems becoming worse despite the best of intentions of all involved. Jesus rejected this blame-based approach to change when he was asked whose sin caused a man to be blind. "Was it his sin or was it his parents?" (John 9:1–3) Rather than entertain the notion of cause or blame, Jesus saw it as a transformational opportunity for the glory of God to be manifest.

At its best, the medical model approach results in incremental change but not in transformation. Transformation occurs primarily when the organization is able to view itself in a very different light. The appreciative approach with its life-giving focus rather than problem-reduction focus opens the possibility of organizational transformation. This approach is consistent with the transformation to the realm of abundant life that Jesus offers. Jesus did not come that we might have less death or less problems; he came that we might have life and share it abundantly with our neighbors.

Any intentional change can be understood as a process of going from an initial state A to a preferred state B. The transition from A to B is achieved by discovering, accessing, and utilizing resources. A resource is anything an individual or group needs to make the change. Resources may be tangible, such as material, equipment, and money, or intangible such as love, motivation, commitment, and a sense of purpose. This model of discovering and using resources to transition from A to B is an elemental pattern for making changes. Large-scale changes are actually a series of nested and chained sets of the basic A-to-B pattern. For example, building a church hall is a large A-to-B that is made up of a series of smaller A-to-B steps such as securing the plans and permits, raising the funds, hiring contractors, purchasing materials, etc. Even within these smaller steps, additional steps from A to B may be needed, such as hiring subcontractors to perform the construction tasks. Each step is achieved through accessing and using resources.

Figure 7.1. The A⟶B Change Model

Intentional transition ministry began as a response to congregations making a change between rectors or senior pastors, especially in settings of congregational turmoil where a subsequent successful ministry was likely to be difficult to achieve. In these situations the transitional minister's task was to help the congregation secure the resources to create a stable foundation for a successful ministry. Over time, stable congregations also found benefit in having an intentional period of ministry to help them manage their transition between clergy.

The skills and strategies learned in helping congregations make these transitions are the same for congregations making other transitions, such as building new buildings, implementing strategic plans, developing ministries, or responding to growth. Rather than limit this understanding of transitions to the change of clergy, the appreciative way looks at managing all transitions from the perspective of the A-to-B change model and how it may be used to create desired outcomes that efficiently use resources and are sustainable over time.

The three steps of managing transitions in this A-to-B model involve

- Knowing where you are starting from;

- Knowing where you are going;

- Locating the resources to achieve the goal.

The first thing you need to be able to make a change is to know where you are starting from. One of the fundamental differences between appreciative inquiry and other organizational development processes is that you do not need to know or have insight into why you are starting at this place or who is to blame for you being at this place in order to create change. This is a radical, counterintuitive idea in a culture that believes gaining insight into antecedent causes is an essential precursor to creating change.

Most organizational development processes put considerable emphasis on understanding the cause of problems, yet it is interesting to note that Jesus does not require people to have insight into the nature of their problems before he embarks on a healing process with them. In the story of the woman at the well, Jesus was not distracted by trying to help the woman understand why she had had several failed relationships. Rather, he used the strategy of ambiguity and confusion to lead her to a place of transformation that resulted in her acknowledgment that Jesus is the Messiah (John 4:7–30).

In addition to rejecting ideas of cause and blame, the appreciative approach is very intentional in deciding what about this starting point is important to know. The change process starts by using shared storytelling to discover the best of the congregation at this starting point. Within these best experiences the core values can be discerned. Using the life-giving best and what is valuable to the congregation as the starting point ensures that there is a solid foundation for creating change and that the changes will be in the direction of greater life and value.

Equally important as knowing your starting point is discovering the goal or the preferred future (Point B) you want to achieve. You and your congregation are going to spend the rest of your life in the future. Ensuring that it is your preferred future is essential to creating vital communities. Planning for and co-creating that preferred future is imperative, or you will simply become the victim of external forces beyond your apparent control.

For many congregations, having a goal related to their core purpose needs to be their first step. From my experience of congregational consulting, very few congregations know their core purpose. In fact, in the past twenty-three years of church consulting I have found parishioners from only two congregations that have been able to clearly articulate their congregation's purpose. Without knowing their God-given purpose and grounding their goals in that purpose, change processes are likely to be random, life-sapping distractions that mire the congregation in mindless mediocrity.

Once the goal has been determined, the resources to achieve the goal need to be located and accessed. As previously noted, these resources may be both tangible and intangible. When an obstacle occurs or the congregation fails to achieve the goal, the task is to remain in the appreciative mode and ask "What other resources do we need?" rather than engage in a process of blame and exploring why the goal was not achieved. Understanding why a goal was not met is simply an exercise in excuse-making and does not help achieve the goal. As the group explores the additional resources to achieve the goal, it may be appropriate to decide that the goal is not achievable because there are insufficient available resources. Such decision-making based on the availability of resources is inherently different from making decisions on the basis of blame and fault-finding.

In leading people through these three steps of change, I find that goal formulation is critically important. Goals must be positively stated and imaginable. It is impossible to work toward a negative goal such as being less depressed or having less conflict. This is typified in St. Paul's great conundrum in the book of Romans. The harder he tries not to do something he despises, the worse it actually gets (Romans 7:15). The solution for St. Paul is to stop focusing on what he doesn't want and to reorient to the grace of God in Jesus that already is. When confronted with a problem or negative goal, people need to transform it into a preferred alternative. Being less depressed becomes growing in happiness. Managing conflict becomes collaboration-building.

In order to accomplish something, you must also be able to imagine the desired outcome. Negatively stated goals are actually impossible to imagine and hold in consciousness. Many social programs fail because they are negatively stated goals that are impossible to imagine realistically. When people are unable to imagine a goal, they will disengage emotionally and simply view the program as an activity for someone else to engage in.

For example, many congregations are working on the United Nations Millennium Development Goals (MDGs) as part of their outreach efforts. While their intention is honorable, many preachers have been frustrated in their efforts to motivate their congregations to engage in these outreach efforts. One reason is the goal is often negatively stated and unimaginable. Consider the goal to reduce poverty by fifty percent. Most people, when asked about their sense of the starting point A, will conjure up a picture in their minds of hungry children. When preachers talk about poverty, they will evoke these images. When preachers call people to work toward reducing the poverty by fifty percent, the people balk. "What does a picture of fifty percent less hungry children look like?" Most people are unable to create a realistic picture of the goal the preacher is calling them to engage in. Because they cannot create that image, they will not commit to the task.

What the preacher needs to do is ask the question, "What would we have if we did not have poverty?" Most people will imagine well-fed, happy children. The next step is to ensure that this goal is imaginable in a way that the parishioners can see themselves realistically working to ensure that children are well-fed and happy. Most people, when asked, cannot realistically imagine every child in the world being well-fed. So the picture needs to be reduced in size through a series of steps until it is imaginable. "Can you imagine every child in America being well-fed?" And if you can't do that, and many people can't, then how about in your city, or in your town? And for those who cannot do that, they may need to get down to "Can you imagine every child on your street being well-fed?" Most people can get down to a place where they can imagine being engaged in ensuring that some children are well-fed.

Once people have that picture in mind and they know they have the resources to achieve it, they will be more willing to engage in the task of ensuring the children in their image are well-fed. Having created that realistic image in their minds, it can be expanded to include some other parts of the world. "So you can imagine every child in your street being well-fed. . . . Can you imagine being part of a program to ensure that every child on a street, in a city, or a town, of Haiti, or Darfur, or some other place, would be well-fed?" Most people can create that picture in mind, having achieved the first picture. Now the person has two imaginable and realistic goals that a group of people doing outreach in a church could actually work toward.

Once the goal has been established, the appreciative inquiry process of shared interviewing and storytelling about best experiences is used to discover the resources needed to achieve the goal. This process is iterative, as the storytelling can also be used to help the congregation create new goals and vision. The preferred approach is to engage all the congregation or stakeholders in the storytelling and visioning process. These events are typically referred to as an "appreciative inquiry summit." By engaging all the stakeholders in the storytelling and visioning process, the community as a whole will own the outcome and be more motivated to engage in achieving the goal than they would if the goal was imposed from an external authority. Basing the preferred future on the collective best of the past also ensures that the images of the future are realistic because they are based on what the community has known to be true in the past and are not based on the disconnected fantasies of a few in the congregation.

Contrary to popular opinion, I believe people do like change, especially when it is a blessing. What they do not like, and will strongly resist, is any change that steals something of value from them. In its simplest form a blessing is receiving something that is of value. For a change to be perceived as a blessing, state B must be of greater value than state A, plus the cost of the resources to achieve the final state. If B is perceived as being of lesser value than A, then the people will resist the change and the outcome will be unsustainable.

In the change literature, considerable emphasis is given to dealing with resistance to change. In most understandings, resistance is a pejorative term used against people who are reluctant or hesitant to embark on a change. I find most of these understandings unhelpful in actually helping people to make changes. From my experience, resistance occurs because part of the congregation is unable to perceive the benefit of the change. In many cases the part that is resisting is actually a wise part that knows the outcome is a curse rather than a blessing. Responding to resistance requires helping the part that is resisting perceive that the change is a blessing. If this is not done, the change will be resisted because it is experienced as an act of violence being inflicted upon them.

In addition to gathering stories of the people's best experiences of their congregation, I also inquire what they value about their congregation and gather stories of when they have experienced these values. One reason I spend time understanding what is valued by the congregation is to ensure that any change is taking the people to a place of greater value and therefore will be perceived as a blessing. Several biblical narratives demonstrate the nature of resistance and the benefit of knowing what people value.

The rich young ruler came to Jesus and asked, "What must I do to have eternal life?" Jesus told him, "Sell everything, give to the poor, and follow me." Here the final state B was following Jesus without his possessions. But the rich young ruler could not perceive that following Jesus was more valuable than having all of his possessions. And so he resisted following Jesus, and walked away full of sorrow (Mark 10:17–22). On the other hand, when Jesus is talking to James and John, he said, "Leave your nets and come follow me" (Matthew 4:19). For whatever reason, James and John understood that following Jesus was more valuable than being fishermen. So they willingly followed Jesus.

The other thing that Jesus did with James and John was to relate following him into their core value of being fishermen. Jesus transformed the nature of being a fisherman from simply fishing for fish, to fishing for people. As James and John followed Jesus they would continue to experience the core essence or value of fishing. It would be manifested differently, but the core value of fishing, and whatever joy and pleasure that they got from fishing, would continue to be theirs as they made that change to following Jesus.

When leading congregations in transition, leaders must ensure that the congregation's narrative is transformed to be consistent with the desired goal. Individuals and organizations know themselves by the meaning they create from the stories they tell about themselves. These personal and corporate narratives become self-confirming labels. Some congregations may have a narrative that says, "We are poor and can't achieve anything," So they remain mired in mediocrity. Other congregations may have a narrative that says, "We can do anything we set our mind to." They will continually be looking for new opportunities to minister to their community. In congregations with little sense of mission or purpose, the narrative may be vague or operating implicitly rather than explicitly in the decision-making in the congregation.

If the narrative remains inconsistent with the goal, the outcome will not be sustainable and the people will return to living and manifesting their former narrative. This is the struggle for Moses in leading the people out of Egypt. The people came out of Egypt with a slave narrative to which they were easily tempted to return (Numbers 11:4–6). It took forty years for the "people of God" narrative to take sustainable root in their consciousness. Within the community there will be many narratives about the past. Rather than working to have a shared *historical narrative*, it is more important to work toward having a shared *future* narrative that the people can live into manifesting in their present.

Jesus was a master at transforming people's narrative to ensure that individual acts of healing and ultimately his entire ministry were sustainable. Jesus ministered to people whose narrative was the oppression of the kingdom of Rome. Yet, in his preaching, Jesus did not talk about resisting Rome, or fighting Rome, or wanting to overthrow Rome, or reducing the power of Rome in their lives. In fact, Jesus said very little about the kingdom of Rome. Rather he changed the narrative from the *kingdom of Rome* to the *Kingdom of God*. If he hadn't changed the narrative to the Kingdom of God, after his death the people would have simply reverted to being oppressed people living under the rule of Rome. But after his death and resurrection, people were aware of the reign of God in their lives, and that became their narrative. When the people said "Jesus is Lord," they were, in part, making a political statement that Nero was not lord and the Romans weren't lord. Now Jesus and the Kingdom of God was the realm in which they were living despite the continuation of the external Roman reality.

To transform their narrative Jesus used stories that the people could relate to and knew to be true. He talked of the Kingdom of

God not as some futuristic kingdom but as a reality that was among them and that they already knew in part. As he focused attention on this kingdom that they already knew in part and would be coming in its fullness, the kingdom's reality grew in their consciousness. Without grounding the coming future in their past and present experience, Jesus would have created an unrealistic fantasy with no power to sustainably transform lives.

Appreciative inquiry is commonly known for its use of interviews and having people sharing stories of their best experiences of their community. The purpose of this storytelling is to transform the congregation's narrative rather than just gathering data or opinions. Many congregations use surveys during transitional times to gather opinions; however, these are of minimal value in transforming a congregation's narrative or motivating people toward a preferred future. Christianity did not flourish because eleven disciples took a vote and ten said they believed in the resurrection. Christianity flourished because people told stories of their encounters with the risen Jesus and how he had transformed their lives.

A congregation cannot change one iota of its past. It can, however, choose which parts of its past it will use as a foundation to build on and inform its future. Within a congregation there are helpful narratives and unhelpful narratives. Both stories are "true" but neither story is absolutely true. Humanity is never completely anything. We are both selfish and kind. Appreciative inquiry wants to call forth the best from people rather than try to get them to do less of their worst. Knowing which stories to tell and framing the "right" questions to engage these stories is essential to liberate the power of the appreciative process. I ask people to tell stories of their best because I want to bring their best to their endeavors. For it is when people are at their best that they are most closely manifesting the image of God that God created them to be. Just as Jesus found the coming Kingdom of God in the people's past and present, we use appreciative storytelling to discover the congregation's future in the life-giving stories of their past and present. When grounded in these stories, the congregation is able to imagine a preferred future that they know is achievable because they have manifested parts of it in the past.

When dealing with problems or negative narratives, there is

little need to spend significant time considering their antecedents or causes just as Jesus spent little time considering the origins of the Roman oppression narrative. In many transitional ministry settings, it has been fashionable to diagnose or label conflicted congregations as pathological. Some congregations have even been labeled "clergy-killers" and stories are gathered and shared to reinforce this narrative. Unfortunately, knowing the origins of this narrative and who is to blame for it will actually reinforce the narrative rather than liberate the congregation into collaborative relationships with clergy. Unless the clergy-killer narrative is transformed, no amount of transitional ministry will be helpful or of value.

There are several steps to transform a negative narrative such as "we are clergy-killers." The first is to consider what is wanted in its place, such as, "We are the people of God, clergy and lay, who collaborate with each other in life-giving ways." In this way the problem is not ignored but transformed into a desired goal. With this goal in mind, the congregation is invited to share stories of times when they have collaborated. Even if these times of collaboration are rare, they must exist for the congregation to have been created and survived despite their apparent problems. These "rediscovered" stories of collaboration are used to create the foundation for the new narrative that can be shared by the congregation.

In contrast to the clergy-killer narrative, congregations that have been badly hurt by clergy abuse may have narratives such as "clergy aren't to be trusted because they are vindictive or hurtful." Unless these narratives are transformed by the remembering of trustworthy clergy or a redemptive experience of a trustworthy pastor, the people will remain untrusting and uncooperative.

While the examples of "clergy-killers" or "congregation-abusers" may be extreme, all congregations have narratives that need to be remembered, owned, and transformed. In the appreciative approach, the focus is on the outcome of the narrative rather than the veracity of the narrative, because all narratives have some element of truth embedded in them. Many congregations have a "we are welcoming" narrative. This narrative is obviously true for those who were welcomed and remained to share in it. On the other hand, people who attended only once and did not feel welcomed do not share in that narrative. Rather than enter into argument and debate over whether the congregation is actually welcoming, the appreciative approach inquires into people's experience of being welcomed. The very telling of those stories will expand the welcoming narrative in consciousness and empower people to replicate them.

The final step of creating a new narrative is to discern the congregation's purpose and embed the new narrative in their larger purpose narrative. As noted earlier, many congregations have little understanding of their purpose; consequently, one of the first steps will be to help the congregation discern their purpose. This is achieved through the intentional use of the appreciative inquiry process of discovering the congregation at their best. The organization's life-giving purpose will be revealed within the common themes of these stories.

In the Gospels, Jesus invites us to remember him in the breaking of bread and sharing the cup of wine. The word "remember" means to *re-member* or put back together in consciousness. In the Eucharist we tell the Jesus story and are put back together in him. Similarly, the remembering and telling of stories of people's best in appreciative processes re-members or puts them back together at their best. It is this best that leaders need to evoke and call forth as their communities engage in the process of transition and transformation, for it is only from their collective best that they can ensure that change will be a life-giving blessing.

A Word of Acknowledgment

In addition to the members of the appreciative inquiry community at large and the numerous participants in my training programs who have challenged and honed my ideas and understanding of the appreciative way, I am particularly grateful to participants in my coaching teleconferences who provided great feedback and editorial advice as this chapter was written.

Notes

1. For a more extensive description of the origins of appreciative inquiry and its application in organizations, see J. Watkins, and B. Mohr,

Appreciative Inquiry: Change at the Speed of Imagination (San Francisco, CA: Jossey Bass/Pfeiffer, 2001).

A briefer, readily accessible description of appreciative inquiry in organizations can be found in S. Hammond, *The Thinbook of Appreciative Inquiry* (Bend, OR: Thinbook Publishing, 1996).

The reader is also referred to the online Appreciative Inquiry Commons at http://appreciativeinquiry.case.edu for a comprehensive virtual library of appreciative inquiry resources.

2. Some variation occurs between authors in the number of Ds and their descriptions. Early models and some authors refer to a 4D model of "discover, dream, design, and deliver." Because the discovery process is dependent on the choice of inquiry topics, I prefer to include "define" as an essential element in appreciative processes.

3. D. L. Cooperrider, "Positive Image, Positive Action: The Affirmative Basis of Organizing," in *Appreciative Management and Leadership* rev. ed., ed. S. Srivasta & D. L. Cooperrider (Euclid, OH: Williams Custom Publishing, 1999), 121.

4. Milton Erickson, MD (1901–80), was a psychiatrist who developed numerous strategies for creating change. People who studied with him went on to develop strategic family therapy, solution-focused therapy, neuro-linguistic programming, self-relations therapy, and also to teach his resource-focused way of joining with people to co-create desired outcomes. To learn more about Milton Erickson and his students, see http://www.erickson-foundation.org.

5. An expanded understanding of the appreciative way can be found in R. J. Voyle and K. M. Voyle, *Core Elements of the Appreciative Way: An Introduction to Appreciative Inquiry for Work and Daily Living* (Hillsboro, OR: Clergy Leadership Institute, 2006).

Chapter 8

HOW CAN WE MAKE PLANS NOW?

Robert E. Friedrich, Jr.

Several years ago at the annual meeting of the Interim Ministry Network (IMN), I proposed that the transitional time between the departure of the last "settled" pastor and the arrival of the next is an ideal time for that congregation to use strategic planning to discern its mission. Since then, I have enjoyed opportunities to facilitate strategic planning both as a consultant to churches in transition and as an interim pastor. The good news is that strategic planning works, and works very well! In almost every case, whether I was serving as consultant or pastor, the congregation announced that strategic planning led to a sense of empowerment and new self-definition.

Strategic planning is a carefully defined process of preparation for the future. Businesssdirectory.com defines strategic planning as the "systematic process of envisioning a desired future, and translating this vision into broadly defined goals or objectives and a sequence of steps to achieve them."[1] While this definition comes from the business world, it works equally well in faith communities. Using a faith-based strategic planning process is the best way to insure that the process stays grounded in the congregation's belief system.

Strategic planning avoids three common pitfalls. First is the "courtship" pitfall. What often passes for search is really courting, on the part of both clergy and search committees. Over thirty-five years of ordained ministry I have behaved exactly as a suitor wooing a partner. I hid my flaws. I found out what it was the church was seeking and presented myself as the one who could do it all. I wrote thank-you notes and engaged in wonderful manners that I didn't really use for anything else. As much as I could hide my faults and weaknesses, they were hidden. As much as I could pump my assets and accomplishments, they were pumped. In short, I did everything to appear the most desirable pastor available. To be honest, it was very close to the way I wooed my wife.

But it was never one-sided. A church looking at me, and thinking it might want to call me, showed me the perfect parish. It is important to remember that, in this setting, all churches say they want to grow. Their harmony and commitment to mission are exemplary.

We all know that churches and pastors do get together, often with a "celebration" service remarkably similar to a wedding. We also know, sometimes in personally painful ways, that pastors and congregations fall out of love. Conflict consultants are called in, denominational resources are committed, and very often a separation is arranged. A 2002 *USA Today* editorial stated that "clergy firings are very high compared with the national labor force, where 1.2% of all employees are involuntarily terminated. The rate is even higher than coaches in the NFL, a notoriously unstable profession."[2]

How remarkably similar to what happens to engaged lovers once the knot is tied! The glamour is replaced with disappointments over money, dishes, toothpaste, and any of many areas of disagreement. We all know about the prevalence of separations and divorces. If there is to be an effective way of conducting a pastoral search, it must be honest and realistic. Engaging in a strategic planning-driven search preparation is the best way I have found to achieve that.

Second, there is the "Moses Up the Mountain" pitfall. It is possible to build a "mission-driven" church around the ideas of one person. Charismatic leaders can build remarkably large and generous followings. They often can be found on television. We have seen them rise. We have seen them fall, hard. The most obvious example at this moment is Saddleback Church, whose pastor, Rick Warren, hammers at being purpose-driven as an individual and a church. "A great purpose statement will provide a specific standard by which you can review, revise, and improve everything your church does."[3] Please note that I do not believe that this ecclesiastical phenomenon is a bad thing or not from God. It is just not the norm in mainline churches. While Warren carefully delineates the process to become "purpose-driven," others derive their purpose from the charisma of the leaders. This can lead to a foundation built on sand, which is unstable and shifts, as the Gospel of Matthew reminds us (Matthew 7:26–27).

The most commonly practiced is probably "the Messiah pitfall." This is the shadow side of the "Moses" pitfall. Congregations tend to mark time during transition. They are afraid to establish new directions because they might not suit the newly called pastor, so they adopt a wait-and-see attitude. Search committees from churches where I was being considered for a call would often proudly tell me that they were holding off on new initiatives until the pastor comes. Similarly, a non-profit service provider for whom I was doing research was holding off on any major decisions until the new CEO arrived. They were anxious about this because their board had picked him and they knew little about him. Yet when that "Messiah" does come and tries to implement a vision, there is great potential for failure because the vision has no roots in the congregation.

In the Episcopal Church, this kind of attitude is sometimes labeled "Father knows best." "Father," the traditional name for the male priest, will come and tell us what to do. "Father" will bring ministry to the church. We will do what ever "Father" says. Of course, the reality is that no one wants to be told by the priest or any one else what to do or what to value. Furthermore, no one person brings ministry or mission to the church. Ministry and mission are embedded in the basic belief system of the church. The role of the congregation is to examine who they are, discover the nature of the world they live in, and then discern the particulars of God's call to them. This will be their plan.

A congregation is well-advised to identify its own top priorities as an integral part of the professionally guided transitional ministry. This avoids the pitfalls mentioned above. Focus is kept on the ministry of the people and the pastor is called to be a partner in a shared vision for ministry.

The process I tend to follow, when done in full, generally takes the following shape. First, appoint a strategic planning task force, whose job is to distill the data, not plan. Next comes ministry assessment where parishioners gather in focus groups. Historical reflection and norms identification are whole parish events. Other steps in the planning include examining outreach opportunities, which can include interviewing key people in the community and using one of the demographic and ethnographic tools available to most churches. Finally, there will be a planning task force and vestry work day, where the goal is to name the final three to five top priorities for the congregation. This information will be incorporated in the congregational profile document and search process.

After the new pastor is called and in place, I encourage a congregational meeting to allow all to reaffirm and claim ownership in the plan. Implementation is the final step. A vestry retreat is held to determine what resources are needed to accomplish the main goals. The vestry and the pastor will work together to equip the congregation for this ministry.

Why engage in strategic planning during the interim? First, strategic planning is good for anybody, at any time. Congregations need to pray for God's guidance. They also need to discern—and then plan for—a vision that reflects the collective wisdom of the congregation. The old axioms are true. People don't plan to fail; they just fail to plan. If you aim at nothing, you'll hit it every time. I offer a new axiom: All churches have a mission; some missions are intentional; others are unintentional. The default unintentional mission is survival; and that leads finally to institutional death.

The process I use involves looking at the congregation's life cycle. It is a pattern that humans, corporations, nations, and congregations all follow: birth to infancy to adolescence to prime to maturity to aristocracy to bureaucracy to remembrance to death as illustrated in the Figure 8.1 on page 94. This is a loose adaptation of work done by the Episcopal Church's Congregational Resources office and by Martin Saarinen in an Alban Institute monograph entitled *The Life Cycle of a Congregation*, and work done for the business sector by Ichak Adizes.[4]

In Figure 8.1, the Interim Ministry Network defines the four letters that mark the characteristics of each stage:

The "E" factor—energizing function. It includes such things as vision and hope, excitement and enthusiasm, and a sense of potency and potentiality. By itself, it has an undifferentiated quality like that of an excited infant whose arms and legs flail around in all directions.

The "P" factor—specific programs and service undertaken by the congregation in response to the needs of its own membership, of its environment, or the ministry mandates of the broader church that it supports. The congregation with a highly developed "P" factor corresponds to the "Body of Christ" image. "P" is located in externals and may cause excitement in the congregation.

The "A" factor—how the **administration** of the congregation developed in the rational domain of the corporate organism. It spells out the conscious intentionality of the congregation in the form of mission statements, goals, objectives, budgets, and planning. It determines how the human and material resources of the congregation can be used most efficiently and effectively in the offering of programs and services, which it deems important in actualizing the vision and fulfilling its mission. The "A" factor serves the functions of coordination and integration.

The "I" factor—**inclusion** relates to both individuals and groups within and outside the congregation. A high "I" congregation tends to image itself as a "fellowship of saints" and its members tend to be drawn by the compassionate and open style of Christ's ministry as depicted in St. Luke's gospel.[5]

In the following diagram, upper-case letters indicate high or a strong characteristic and lower-case letters denote low:

E = high energy, e = low energy.

P = high program, p = low program.

A = high administration, a = low administration.

I = high inclusion, i = low inclusion

At birth, institutions begin with high energy and little else. Mark the monumental efforts of successful church starters. Infants add inclusion needs. Adolescents have high program needs. At prime, we are firing on all four cylinders. At maturity, we feel good but the energy is draining. At administration, program drops away

Where are we in our congregation's life cycle?

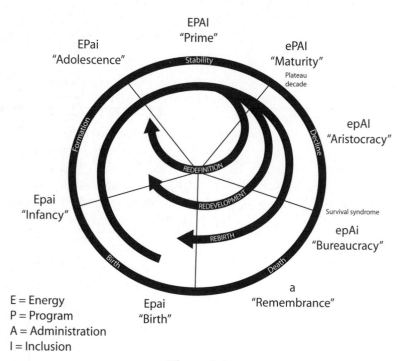

Figure 8.1

and management takes an even higher place. In bureaucracy, only administration is left. Witness high-endowment, low-attendance congregations with large staffs and little else. In remembrance and death, only a little administration is needed to remember the history of the closed institution.

The danger point follows immediately on the heels of prime. In maturity, we delude ourselves into thinking that we still are in prime. We are as yet only dimly aware that reserves of strength are waning. This is the position of a host of churches. Congregations that thrived with the baby boomers, sometimes into the 1980s or 1990s, are now noticing the graying of hair and the dwindling of youth group and Sunday School.

An American Baptist church with which I consulted provides an example of this process. I gathered the leadership board and the task force together in a kickoff retreat. We reviewed the process, looked at creative tension, the meaning of size, and the life cycle of a congregation. I presented each participant with their own two copies of the life cycle of a congregation as described above.

Following explanation, I asked the thirteen participants to mark privately where they saw their church in its life cycle. I then took them and marked their Xs on a single page. The group gasped and experienced an "aha!" moment when I collected all thirteen and recorded each person's assessment. Everyone saw their congregation on the downhill side—declined down to aristocracy, past prime, and even survival. Figure 8.2 shows their responses. I was pleased that their report to the congregation led to earnest commitment to seeing the parish through to rebirth and redevelopment.

Having gained clarity about their situation, they asked me, "What can we do?" My answer was, "Engage in strategic planning!"

Strategic planning during the interim has biblical precedent. The book of Acts gives a good model of strategic planning. In Acts 15 we read about the first church council, where the congregation and its leaders decide on a plan which "seems good to the Holy Spirit and to us" (Acts 15:28). That is incarnational, saying, "God and we decided to do this. . . ." Dare we hope for a plan that is both human and divine? I think we don't dare to do less. And that will require more work and more prayer and more time than go into strategic planning in the business world.

Transition time is the ideal time to evaluate the effectiveness of our ministry because we are not just trying to make sense of change, we are looking at ourselves and our ministry and trying to plan for a future. A benefit to strategic planning in the interim is that it provides ways to work on the five developmental tasks of interim ministry and provides information to use in the congregational profile. Let's take a look at how strategic planning can help the congregation in its work on the developmental tasks.

First, *we are able to connect to new leadership and directions.* Our goal is to determine the top four mission priorities for this parish over the next four years and to phrase them in a way that

Where are we in our congregation's life cycle?

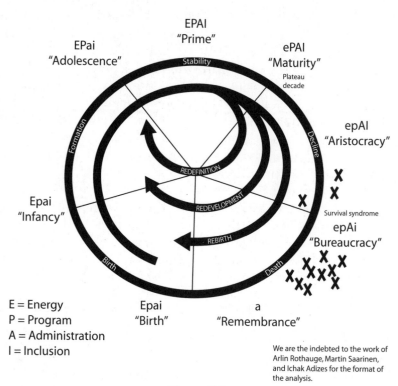

EPAI
"Prime"

EPai
"Adolescence"

ePAI
"Maturity"

Stability

Plateau
decade

epAI
"Aristocracy"

Formation

Decline

REDEFINITION

Epai
"Infancy"

REDEVELOPMENT

Survival syndrome

epAi
"Bureaucracy"

REBIRTH

Birth

Death

E = Energy
P = Program
A = Administration
I = Inclusion

Epai
"Birth"

a
"Remembrance"

We are the indebted to the work of
Arlin Rothauge, Martin Saarinen,
and Ichak Adizes for the format of
the analysis.

Figure 8.2

makes sense in a parish description for the search process. We will ask ourselves: What strengths do we want to enhance? What in our corporate life needs repair? What is our immediate and obvious outreach opportunity? What are the hopes, dreams, and aspirations that we have seen fulfilled, that, by the grace of God, we will do now?

To accomplish this, we will employ prayer to ascertain the will of God in the ministry of this church. Our final goals will include God and as many parishioners as possible. Members will be invested in the results, which will be used in the call process.

Second, *we come to terms with our history.* The all-parish historical exercise is a proven way to recognize the events in our corporate past, the trends that emerge, and the meaning of what is important. At this event we tell stories of the past, sometimes learning new perspectives about long-ago events. Old wounds are allowed to heal. Past failures can be mourned and successes celebrated.

Third, *we examine leadership and organizational needs.* Looking at our values and norms helps us to understand our congregation and then to communicate this to pastoral candidates. Ministry assessment looks at what we are doing and how we are doing. I prefer focus groups ("fireside chats" or "cottage meetings") because the ubiquitous written parish survey lacks personal and corporate responsibility. Focus groups encourage dialogue and taking ownership of one's opinions. Mission/outreach exploration identifies our opportunities and lets us discern our unique calling, preferably in our own neighborhood.

Fourth, *we develop a new identity and image.* This developmental task is sometimes rejected by those who embrace the comfortable familiarity of the past. Even though they know things don't stay the same, they try to hold onto old ways of doing and being. A planning process that involves the entire congregation and moves slowly allows for the gradual realization that change is larger than the loss of pastor or whatever the change event was. Such a planning process helps the people to understand that the new identity is naming the current reality. The strategic planning process makes this discovery its whole aim.

Fifth, *we connect with the denomination.* Even the most loosely connected denominations find the judicatory is helpful during transition. It is good for the congregation to renew its identity as Presbyterian or Baptist or UCC. Part of the strategic planning process will be for the congregants to reflect about what it means to be a member of this particular denomination at this time. They will learn how denominational polity impacts their planning for the future. They will discover denominational resources to help them in their planning process.

When a congregation uses the transition time to define their mission plan, they will understand who they are and who God is calling them to be. This self-understanding will be reflected in the profile document. They will be ready for a new future, which will be a choice, not a reaction to the past. This congregation will call clergy who are eager and able to lead a direction chosen by the congregation and endorsed by the clergyperson.

I have had opportunity to guide congregations of varying denominations through this process in their transition time, both as transitional pastor and as a consultant. One congregation I served provides another case study. It grew out of a "total ministry" tradition, with every member a minister and only part-time service by ordained ministers. This is laudable, but this parish was situated in a high-growth urban area and some of the leadership saw the need for a full-time rector. I came on for a designated two-year time period. After spending the first nine months on trust-building, stewardship, and building issues, we launched into a program of strategic planning designed to feed into the search process.

The leadership, vestry, and a task force were energized and focused by the kickoff retreat where we looked at size, creative tension, life cycle, polarities, and process. Particularly enlightening was determining the priorities around whether to have a full-time clergyperson or not. A polarity exercise helped them visualize the upside and downside of this, their central question.[6] Figure 8.3 shows how this worked.

All the positives of having a rector they placed in the L+ quadrant. They are good, but they have downsides, which are in the L- quadrant. I asked, what can we do to counteract these negatives? The advantages to having no rector are in the R+ quadrant. But these too have downsides, and they are listed in R-. Back to L+. The arrow directions eventually form the mathematical sign for infinity:

Indeed the argument could go on infinitely. The parish had to realize it needed to decide one way or another and agree to live with both the positives and negatives.

L+

- Trained leadership
- Consistency
- Presence
- Direction
- Comfort
- Challenge
- Pastoral care
- Education

Rector

R+

- Less $$$
- Lay control
- More lay participation

No Rector

Easy

- Expensive
- Quirks
- Lower participation
- Less lay control
- Direction can change
- Discomfort
- Difficult selection
- May disagree with him/her

L-

Hard

- Burnt-out staff
- Burnt-out everyone
- Chaos
- No captain
- Confusing to newcomers
- No continuity

R-

Figure 8.3

When the congregation met to identify the parish norms, many were able to see the places where conflict was inevitable unless their pattern of punishing leadership by withholding giving changed. Looking at demographic and ethnographic trends in the church's geographical sphere of influence led to ideas for outreach. In time, the vestry and leadership sifted down to their four top priorities and goals: "outreach and good works; reconciliation, fellowship, and the presence of the Holy Spirit; evangelism; and passionate Christianity." At a later date they were able to name more specific details of each goal. In addition, they also realized that their manner of relating to each other had to change. After I left, they called a half-time rector.

A particularly effective job was done by a large, wealthy Episcopal congregation that had a long and proud history. The first step was a Friday evening and Saturday kick-off retreat for the vestry and the strategic planning task force. The Congregational Systems Inventory (CSI) was the center piece of this event.[7] The first event in the retreat was an explanation of family system theory. I like to use PowerPoint presentations and an LCD projector, though it is by no means required. I explained, "We'll be thinking of our congregation as a *system*. We humans fall into set ways of doing things ("my pew," "we've always done it that way"). Systems theorists call this tendency of people in relationships to develop patterns and keep doing things in the same way "homeostasis." Once an organization or system gets in motion, it tends to keep going in the same way. Just the right amount of tension brings health, but we all find comfort applying familiar solutions to problems. Pushing harder and harder on familiar solutions while fundamental problems persist or worsen is a reliable indicator of non-systemic thinking; e.g., the "what we need here is a 'bigger hammer' syndrome."

Participants filled out the questionnaire in advance so I could collate the results. Together we looked at congregational profile and observed trends. Because three-fourths of the population thinks in tactile as opposed to conceptual terms, I laid a long tape line on the carpet, marked 0 to 10. Then I asked them to actually stand on the place on the tape line where their score came out in each of the categories: strategy, authority, process, pastoral leadership, relatedness, lay leadership, and learning. Then I asked them to look at each category. "Compare and contrast. Lay leaders, do your clergy see themselves as you do? What are the surprises? Clergy, are you near where the rest saw you? Are you surprised by others' impressions?" Participants saw the similarities and differences—amongst laity, and between laity and clergy—in ways that shed light and understanding.

The next retreat event was to walk these leaders through the process to come. I explained that our goal will be to determine the top four mission priorities for this church over the next four years. In the process we certainly want to include God and as many members as possible. The congregation commits itself to pray and work. When we are finished, we want to have members "invested" in the results because they have had ownership in the process.

We asked ourselves: What strengths do we want to enhance? What in our corporate life needs repair? What is our immediate and obvious outreach opportunity? What are our hopes, dreams, and aspirations? We will use something like what I call the "four in four in four in four" rule: We want to discern the top four priorities for the next four years answering the four questions—strengths, repair, mission, dreams—and meeting the four criteria for SPAM goals: specific, personal, attainable, measurable. To accomplish this, we will employ prayer to ascertain the will of God in the ministry of this church and use information gathered from the congregation. It's like making maple syrup—distilling liquid gold from gallons of sap.

I explained that by the time the strategic planning process is finished, we will have engaged the congregation in discernment and prayer, working toward an agreed mission plan by means of leadership retreat, focus groups, historical reflection, norms (values) identification, and ethnographic neighborhood mission study.[8]

We will have distilled observations, revelations, and opinions into tentative goal statements, clarified these into four top mission priorities for this congregation for the next four years. Because this is part of the interim process, we will feed this into the work of the search committee and calling committee. We hope that the congregation and new settled pastor together will develop a clear and comprehensive plan to implement these goals, and then gather the commitment of the congregation into ministry teams for accomplishment of these goals.

The retreat participants looked at their congregation's life cycle. While not as dire a combined view as that of the Baptist church described earlier, it was clear to the group that their parish was on the downward side, and that redevelopment and even rebirth were necessary. Figure 8.4 illustrates their results.

The seven members of the strategic planning task force worked with me, preparing to lead focus groups, twenty "cottage meetings," mostly in homes, where they engaged each group of six to ten parishioners in discussing what is going well here, and what concerns us? Answers were carefully recorded on newsprint. The message was clear: no one's views would be ignored.

The task force distilled all of the accumulated information into this statement: "Cottage meeting themes are these: worship and music are strengths; facilities and fellowship are strengths and weaknesses; communication is a weakness."

The congregation digested this and then gathered for an evening of historical reflection. Sheets of newsprint with an outline of the church's history were hung on the wall and then those present filled in with their comments. The task force reported these themes that emerged from the event: "desire for sense of cohesion; concern about lack of trust; desire for integration of spiritual and intellectual life; concern about communication and leadership."

The congregation next gathered for an evening of norms identification. I introduced it by saying that we would look at six kinds of norms. Every parish has unwritten rules related to the following topics:

Children—How are they viewed and treated? What behavior is expected of children and parents? What does our adult space say about our attitude toward them? What does our child space say about our attitude toward them?

Men/Women—How are they treated the same? How are they treated differently? What behavior is expected of men that is different from that expected of women? What expectations are positive and what expectations are negative?

Conflict—How are differences of opinion dealt with or resolved? What confrontational behavior is expected? What topics are "taboo"? With whom can you disagree and with whom can you not disagree?

Money—How much (amounts) are people expected to give? How is money managed and spent? Who decides? Which efforts have higher priority than others?

Treatment of Clergy—How are clergy addressed? How well are they paid? What behavior is expected of them and of their family? Where are they expected to be taken seriously and where not?

Where are we in our congregation's life cycle?

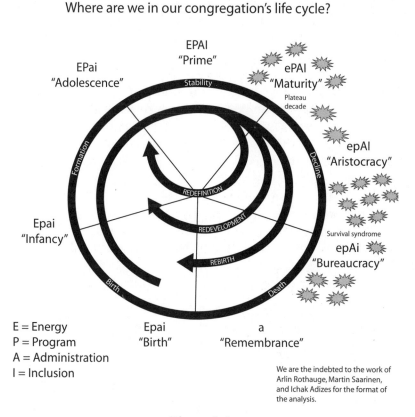

E = Energy
P = Program
A = Administration
I = Inclusion

We are the indebted to the work of
Arlin Rothauge, Martin Saarinen,
and Ichak Adizes for the format of
the analysis.

Figure 8.4

Newcomers—Who talks to them? What behavior is expected of them? What limits are placed on their power? To what extent are their foibles forgiven? What kinds of people are more acceptable in this parish than others?

Groups separated out to consider each area, then reported back to the whole group. The task force later distilled results into the following statements:

1. We don't do conflict well.

2. We don't know where to take dissenting opinions when we disagree with decisions being made by vestry or clergy.

3. Concern about spending our endowment just to maintain the status quo—not for growth.

Norms identification often brings hot issues to the fore where they can be identified and dealt with. I recommended that because the congregation was a fairly anxious system, and because members were almost embarrassed by the negative, even rude, treatment of some by others, a hiatus could occur during which the parish worked on a "behavioral covenant."

They did this, and about six months later, we continued examining outreach possibilities. Task force members interviewed local civic leaders. Together with the congregation, they studied demographic information obtained from Percept, Inc.[9] Particularly valuable were two Context reports, one based on a wider catchment area and the other on the immediate vicinity of the church building.[10]

At the conclusion of their study they agreed:

1. We are similar to our neighbors in education, family structure, and prevalent generation.

2. We differ from our neighbors with regard to the degree of diversity in each population and our preference for spiritual development rather than recreational programs.

3. Community needs are parking, money, senior outreach, and theological education.

At the distillation retreat, the vestry and task force took time for biblical reflection, silence, and a meal. Signs for each item were taped to the wall so that participant could vote by standing by the sign each chose. In its report to the vestry, the task force outlined the four goals:

1. Strengths to enhance

Worship: We will expand our liturgical and musical program.

Buildings: We will preserve and strengthen our heritage of beautiful and historic church buildings.
People: We will recognize the passion and dedication of members of the congregation.

2. What in our corporate life needs repair?

Newcomer integration: We will commit our financial resources to improve the welcome and integration of newcomers.
Conflict: In the conflict that has arisen in our congregation, we have not communicated well with each other, resulting in divisiveness, mistrust of leadership, and discord. We will establish a code of conduct to guide our interactions with one another.
Christian formation and spiritual growth: We will develop and fund a strong program of spiritual formation that invites people of all ages into a lifelong relationship with and commitment to following the way of Christ.
Pastoral care: We will broaden our pastoral care ministry.

3. Immediate and obvious outreach opportunities

Revitalize our approach to outreach: We will commit ourselves to outreach ministries grounded in prayer and study.

4. Hopes and dreams

Stay on course: Once a plan has been adopted, the church leadership will stay the course with funding, energy, and follow-up assessment: We will call a new rector who embraces our plan. Our parish will unite around the vision of the future described by the plan. We will develop effective strategies to fund our plan.

This statement, with further explanatory sub-goals, was an integral part of the search document presented to every candidate and remained an outline for next steps at the call of the rector. For many months it was posted in entirety on the parish's website.

Is there a downside to doing strategic planning in the interim time? Yes, because doing this calls forth a strength that may be healthy and life-giving, or it may be threatening. That strength is empowerment. The following example shows planning gone wrong.

After spending six months helping a church in transition to stabilize, I helped them launch strategic planning. The strategic planning task force was picked and consisted partly of newer members to the congregation. At the kick-off retreat, everyone present went home with a sense of empowerment and new hope for their dwindling, aging, but well-endowed parish.

Unfortunately, two people did not attend the retreat. These people had served as gate-keepers in the congregation. They had, with the departed rector, run the church by deciding ahead of each vestry meeting every matter—even, I was told, down to how many rolls of toilet paper to purchase. The vestry said it felt like a rubber stamp and wondered about its purpose. Beginning planning helped them to see their purpose and they began to exercise it. Unfortunately, the former power group felt threatened enough to complain to a diocesan official, who also had a stake in the old leadership style. Together they arranged to begin the search process immediately, thereby cutting off the new-found moral muscle.

This example shows that it is essential for all the power players to be present when important decisions are made. The clear vision of hindsight suggests that the first priority should have been working on trust and bringing the two groups together so that effective planning could take place. If this divide in the leadership could not be bridged, then consultation with the judicatory is needed.

Like any bold venture, move forward with confidence, be wise, and be observant to see dangerous developments and meet them.

To sum up, strategic planning is helpful during transition because it:

- Makes the church ready for a full-time pastor;

- Enables a high degree of honesty in the search process;

- Opens the congregation to leading of the Holy Spirit;

- Frees the congregation from harmful dependence on clergy;

- Leads the congregation into self-discovery;

- Enables prospective pastors to accurately see the congregation as it is and where it is headed.

Will this affect the deployment process? Yes. Is it worth it? Yes, because it enhances the deployment process, and thus the entire church and its clergy are better served.

Notes

1. http://www.businessdictionary.com/definition/strategic-planning. html (accessed February 10, 2009)

2. Gerald Zelizer, "Revolving Clergy Harms Religion," *USA Today*, February 21, 2002, http://www.usatoday.com/news/opinion/2002/02/21/ ncguest1.htm (accessed February 10, 2009).

3. Rick Warren, *The Purpose-Driven Church* (Grand Rapids, MI: Zondervan, 1995), 101.

4. "Growth and Development," http://www.episcopalchurch.org/ growth_23206_ENG_HTM.htm?menupage=61609; Martin Saarinen, *The Life Cycle of a Congregation*, Alban No. OL124 Digital Download at http://www.alban.org/bookdetails.aspx?id=3540 (accessed February 10, 2009).

5. Martin Homan, ed., *Fundamentals of Transitional Ministry* (Baltimore, MD: Interim Ministry Network, 2005), 93.

6. This method is based on the work of Barry Johnson, *Polarity Management: Identifying and Managing Unsolvable Problems* (Amherst, MA: Human Resource Development Press, 1996).

7. CSI is explained in George Parsons and Speed B. Leas, *Understanding Your Congregation as a System* (Herndon, VA: Alban Institute,

1993). The CSI questionnaire and manual are available through Alban Institute: http://www.alban.org/bookdetails.aspx?id=1178&terms=csi &rawsearchtype=1&fragment=false&SearchType=AndWords (accessed February 10, 2009).

8. The following is an adaptation of a method described in the book I wrote with Roy M. Oswald, *Discerning Your Congregation's Future: A Strategic and Spiritual Approach* (Herndon, VA: Alban Institute, 1996).

9. Since 1987, Percept (http://www.perceptgroup.com) has supplied churches and denominational agencies with demographic and ethnographic resources to help them engage in mission within their particular context. It integrates information about the religious attitudes, preferences, and behavior of the population in the geographic area that you choose as your sphere of influence.

10. See http://www.perceptgroup.com/Products/Context/Contextfront.aspx (accessed February 10, 2009).

SECTION II

STORIES OF TRANSITIONAL MINISTRY

Chapter 9

WHEN THE ENVIRONMENT CHANGES, CHURCH CHANGES

BEN HELMER

Headlines and economics often result in transitional changes for the church. I recently worked with two such transitions in locations separated by 8,000 miles. The Episcopal Diocese of Louisiana comprises the eastern half of the state of Louisiana. The headline that changed it forever was the arrival of Hurricane Katrina in late August 2005. An ocean away, the Episcopal Church in Micronesia (ECIM) is a group of four congregations, three on Guam and one on Saipan—islands of the Northern Marianas in the Western Pacific. Significant economic changes confront Guam, population 160,000, with the impending relocation of 8,000 United States Marines and their dependents from Okinawa beginning in 2010. Guam continues to be the "tip of the spear" for U.S. defense forces in the Pacific. The tranquil island of Saipan has been through a boom-and-bust cycle of garment industries that employed Filipino guest workers. This industry has largely collapsed due to changes in world trade, but many of the Filipino workers remain.

In late August 2005 I was in my seventh year of employment as a staff officer at the Episcopal Church Center in New York with responsibility for rural and small-community ministries. I recall sitting in the living room of the Brooklyn rectory where I stayed, watching the malevolent eye of Katrina come ashore between Mississippi and Louisiana, thinking how terrible it would be, and grateful I was not to be affected by the storm.

A week later I traveled to Guam to assist the Church in Micronesia with some congregational asset mapping and mission planning. I enjoyed those five days, which included a short trip to nearby Saipan. The islands are lovely, inhabited by a racially and culturally diverse population that is reflected in the churches. I returned with the hope that someday I could go back for longer.

In mid-October I met with Bishop George Packard to reflect on my visit to Guam and Saipan. I recall telling him I would be willing to return there should an opportunity for a longer stay be helpful. He thanked me and then told me he had something else in mind. He handed me a letter from Louisiana's Bishop Charles Jenkins, who asked for a chaplain to come for six months to a year to help the diocese during its recovery from Katrina. I said, "But Bishop Packard, I don't have any disaster experience." He smiled and said, "Ben, I think it's time you did!"

After a brief transition through Thanksgiving at home in Missouri, I left with a car and a few essentials for Louisiana. The gracious people at St. James' Episcopal Church in Baton Rouge had arranged temporary housing. I had no contract, no job description. I didn't know anyone there well. I had never been involved in any disaster recovery. While I had been in New York on September 11, 2001, and had gone through my own recovery from that day with the help of many friends and family, my only experience with Ground Zero had been as a volunteer taking coffee to workers one evening in October 2001.

I knew I would encounter things that would simply disarm me, but I had no idea how I would respond to seeing wholesale devastation. From my years as a parish priest I had learned that many times when people have their world seemingly destroyed, all they want is someone there to tell them they will be okay, to pray with them, and listen to them. Somehow, that didn't seem enough preparation for this kind of work.

I also knew that clergy are sometimes the least able to manage their own recovery when their world is shaken. We are good at denial, blaming, or just leaving the scene. I remember hearing that nearly half the parochial clergy left South Florida after Hurricane Andrew in 1992.

In Baton Rouge I was warmly welcomed by the family in whose guesthouse I was to stay. They had watched the peripheral storm effects of Katrina from the windows of their home. When I asked if they had been to New Orleans, they recoiled in horror. Why go there? It was terrible, they said. No, they'd stay home and do what they could, offering housing to evacuated clergy.

Monday, my first day on the job, I arrived at the relocated diocesan offices at St. James' annex in downtown Baton Rouge. Most of the staff was working in what was dubbed the "mosh pit": a large windowless room with folding chairs and assorted tables on which computers were installed. The bishop and his two deputies were in New Orleans and nobody knew I was coming. But Miss Harriet greeted me graciously and two of the staffers took me to lunch. What was I here to do? Well, that certainly was the question.

After two days of trying to look busy—one can only read the same e-mails so many times—I asked for a clergy list and started calling. The results were surprising. Most people remembered I had attended their hastily called clergy conference in October, but none knew I was coming back. Several were eager for appointments with me in New Orleans, a place I had yet to visit.

A trip to New Orleans in November 2005 was like driving into a war zone. Nobody can adequately prepare one to see so much destruction: The exterior skin of the Superdome roof partially peeled back; abandoned cars piled under highway overpasses; buildings buckled and twisted; houses askew; debris piled everywhere; street signs and landmarks washed away; and a general dull gray moldiness on everything. It was obvious as I drove into downtown that it would take many, many months to restore. When I stopped at a store for directions, the clerk, who had lost everything but her job, said she was lucky, but then said of her neighborhood, "it's too broke to fix." That comment would return to me many times in the months to come.

What was obvious to me about post-Katrina New Orleans was that everyone was trying to patch up something to make it look normal. Any building that could be even partially restored, any pieces of familiar things, were being used in an attempt to make something look better. As I began listening to clergy who had lost homes and whose churches were severely damaged, I remembered a quote from a recent documentary about a rural church soon to be closed and removed to a museum site: "Objects and places have more of a hold on us than we realize or imagine." This described New Orleans, a city that had become largely deserted, where landmarks were being gutted and razed every day, and where people were strangers in their own hometown; where objects they had known and places they had gone were lost—some forever.

Guilt began to emerge in some of those who had first felt lucky; guilt because they still had homes and jobs. I expressed my own awkwardness about not being a victim, and was reminded firmly that it was important to have normal people around and that I could be listener and healer precisely because I wasn't a victim.

In the evenings back in Baton Rouge where my family had now joined me, I often spoke with my mother-in-law who had moved to Louisiana with us. She had gone through the blitz in London during World War II. While she admitted what kept her going was often anger at the Nazis, she also told me how difficult it was to see buildings destroyed, homes razed because they were unsafe after a raid, and displaced people wandering around wearing dazed expressions. People in New Orleans were suffering the same losses of familiar places, including spiritual places like their churches.

Grace Church on Canal Street was a flooded shell when I first saw it. The church and rectory had both been under several feet of water for many days, so contents were ruined, walls were decaying with mold; the congregation scattered, many never to return. Yet even with this daunting devastation, the rector and a few remaining parishioners were holding weekly services and making plans to renovate the church and rectory. Another church, St. Luke's, a Caribbean-American congregation, was usable, but only because it had been spared deep water. Pews had to be removed, and the administrative wing was totally gutted after water poured in through the leaky roof.

The congregation at St. Luke's demonstrated the importance of the spirituality of place as they gathered each Sunday. Some returned monthly from as far away as Atlanta to see family and to go to church. Miss Elvia, the warden, was constantly praising their devotion. One Sunday, a ninety year-old man returned and the congregation was ecstatic to see him. As I watched the congregation rebuild little by little while the building restoration progressed, I realized this was a place that gave people hope. As the church was restored, so was part of their lives. The diocesan effort to get churches back to life was a well-conceived effort to restore the spiritual community and heal their souls.

Meanwhile, the work of the Office of Disaster Response, organized shortly after the hurricane, was becoming more complex and demanding. Additional folk were hired, many of them young and inexperienced but willing to put in long hours supervising volunteers, getting materials to the site for gutting homes, keeping people housed, and providing for their own well-being. Weekly staff meetings were a must. At first we only did business; before long I suggested that these times needed to include some open and frank discussions about how everyone was feeling, airing frustrations and anger, with time for prayer and healing ministry. I always attended the meetings and made sure everyone had a chance to describe how they felt. Church meetings are sometimes too heavily controlled when it comes to expressing feelings, and I believe everybody needed a safe place to vent. The supervisors were mostly grateful for the feedback, and as our staff grew to over thirty employees, it was obvious we needed time for community building as well as business.

Toward the middle of 2006, I became aware that the Diocese of Louisiana must change dramatically if it were to remain an effective church. It had literally been blown and washed from a somewhat fussy, traditional, Anglo-Catholic institution to something that would be more dynamic and focused on mission. Bishop Jenkins realized this early on, and by the time we found ourselves almost a year post-Katrina, the "new normal"—as it was being called —included a staff of case workers deployed by the diocese out of several locations, a housing venture called the Jericho Road Project, and a lot of new faces. When we got together as a staff with both the reopened office in New Orleans and the continuing Baton Rouge location, we always had to introduce new people. In the midst of chaos and great obstacles, a revitalized sense of mission to those outside the Episcopal Church was in the air. I began to sense it was time I moved on.

On one of my last trips to New Orleans, I saw the Superdome roof had been repaired and a pro football game was scheduled with the Saints in a few days. Neighborhoods that had been deserted, especially at night, were coming back; stores and restaurants were reopening, and traffic was more evident with local people out and about. The city would live, but it will never be the same.

As I reflect on my year's experience with the diocese, I realize the tremendous power of God to redeem disasters in partnership with the church and volunteers from all over the world. I have seen people cry and rage in frustration over trying to get their homes repaired, then turn to help others who needed it more than they did. I have been part of groups of people who had previously known each other only on a polite social level, but who had now developed deeper bonds of respect and affection through suffering a common disaster. I watched and shared in the beginning transformation of a bishop and a diocese from a rather quiet traditional life to an active and dynamic proclamation of the social gospel among the poor of New Orleans and southern Louisiana.

For myself, I learned I could look at the worst things nature and human folly can bring, and still get up in the morning and go back because the church was there. I was not alone in my stumbling and sometimes faulty approaches to people and their needs. I learned I could be tired but still energized by the ideas of others, and at other times offer them my energy when theirs was failing. The recovery was all about community. Folks who tried to be stars in their approach to things seldom got much done, especially when it was all about them. The rest of us together, trudging along together, saying our prayers together, trying to restore something of normal life, were getting someplace.

I also learned, and hope I shall never forget, that in a disaster it is the poor who always suffer the most. I went to several secular meetings where people said things like "Well, they should take advantage of the resources that are offered," while the poor sat there bewildered at how to access them without car, public transportation, or even telephone. The church offered them hope by treating them with dignity and worth while providing access to resources.

I was taught the value of having an outsider come to help: someone less likely to get caught up in his or her own victimization. People need a self-differentiated person who can move among them, assure them of confidentiality while showing care and concern. They need a coach to help them stay in community when it is much easier to become isolated. They need someone to pray with them and for them when they cannot. They need someone whose schedule isn't full, and who has time available to visit and listen.

Jane, my wife, was able to spend significant time as a volunteer working with a diocesan mobile relief unit in the Lower Ninth Ward, a place many feared to go. Day after day people came for some simple food—they had no electricity or water to prepare meals—and a chance to visit. Often they were dressed in their Sunday best. They were radiant, even joyful in their outlook. They had nothing, but what little we gave was enough, and they were grateful. Whenever I think of New Orleans and remember it in my prayers, I see the faces of those people and know that one day all will be well.

After six months back in our home in West Missouri, Jane and I left for an entirely different kind of assignment. Bishop Packard had invited me to be interim archdeacon, a title only Anglicans could invent, for the Episcopal Church in Micronesia for eighteen months.

We arrived in early June 2007 and quickly became residents of Dededo, the largest village on Guam. Guam is a place of interesting cultural mix: native Chamorro and naturalized Filipinos dominate the social and governmental institutions. But there are also significant numbers of Koreans, Japanese, other Asians, and Micronesians that make up the population. The Roman Catholic Church has by far the majority of members of the faith community.

ECIM has a fifty-year history on Guam, growing from one to three congregations, a pre-K through twelfth grade day school with 550 students, and a mission on Saipan consisting mainly of Filipino guest workers. At one time ECIM was directly connected with the Episcopal Diocese of Hawaii, but for the last two decades it has been part of the extra-provincial Episcopal Church and under the Office of the Bishop Suffragan for Chaplaincies.

My job was to assess the ECIM for a future with less dependence on salaried clergy, and help it begin to take full responsibility for its own mission and ministry. The dependency on full-time clergy had left its mark on ECIM.

Until 2006, the model used was one church/one priest. St. John's, the original congregation, shared its priest with the school until a lay chaplain was hired. St. Michael's, a largely northern Filipino congregation in Dededo, was fairly new and had erected their building under the direction of a full-time Filipino priest. St. Andrew's, in Agat, also engaged a full-time priest and was attended mostly by people originally from the Philippine Independent Church.

Anyone familiar with the costs of professional clergy knows that in recent years they have become increasingly expensive, particularly with escalating health insurance costs. Meanwhile on Guam everything has to be shipped in, so the cost of living is already at least 25 percent higher than on the U.S. mainland. Clergy who come to Guam from the mainland seldom stay longer than a few years, with an expensive relocation cost at either end of their tenure. It was obvious that economics would soon require fewer paid clergy serving the ECIM. A different way of doing ministry had to be found.

After I had been on Guam a few months, I asked several long-time church members why they thought people seemed so indifferent to clergy coming and going. It was obvious from the answers I got that people had stopped investing themselves in relationships and new ideas with clergy who came and then often left abruptly. For those who have lived here for many years, it is difficult to understand the hardships for clergy who come six to eight thousand miles from their familiar homes and must adapt to a culture and climate often very different from their own.

I decided to apply several strategies and see which might help the congregations become less dependent on full-time clergy leadership. I also determined that prayer and scripture would form the basis for anything we did together. The structure of ECIM is simple. A council of advice meets monthly to consider actions for the common welfare of the mission, and each congregation has its own bishop's committee that meets, albeit irregularly. These would be the venues for our talks about mission—the primary strategy I wanted to have conversation about.

In November 2007, ECIM mission strategy got a boost when Presiding Bishop Katharine Jefferts Schori offered to spend Thanksgiving with us after a visit to North Korea. Her presence was uplifting as was her challenge to each of the churches to consider their mission to the people around them. This was new language for some, and this challenge gave me a platform to continue talks about our common mission and each congregation's specific ministry to its neighbors.

The second strategy I chose to encourage was that of partnership. It's difficult to be partners when you're separated by distance. But the ECIM churches on Guam have a good relationship with each other, so I encouraged them to talk together about their needs and to help one another along.

On our way to Guam we had stayed two nights in Honolulu and met with Bob Fitzpatrick, the recently ordained Bishop of Hawaii. He was very interested in pursuing a partnership with ECIM, and made good his promise by visiting in the summer of 2008, installing the new head of St. John's School, and offering the assistance of his Commission on Ministry to help us move two ECIM candidates forward to ordination. For their part, Guam sends at least two people to the annual diocesan convention on Hawaii where ECIM visitors always receive a warm welcome.

In addition to offers of partnership, we looked at the new strategic plan the Diocese of Hawaii was developing and decided to implement a plan of our own that would mirror their major goals. Through telephone calls and eventually real-time conversations on the Web, we began to build our own confidence in planning the future of the ECIM.

In the spring of 2008 an invitation came to send several people to a visitors' weekend in the Diocese of Wyoming. That diocese wanted to showcase its Shared Ministry strategy, a method that includes as many people as possible in the vital worship and pastoral ministry of their congregations. Through Wyoming's generous offer to help with travel expenses, ECIM sent three people to what proved to be a strategic event. They returned with a vision of how each of our churches can be revitalized without full-time clergy, and brought resources to help the congregations move forward.

The third strategy I wanted to implement was renewal and spiritual growth as a foundation for mission. The churches all expressed some desire for this, but trying to get people to take responsibility for it was quite another thing. One leader offered to plan a weekend retreat that worked well, despite obstacles and the unwillingness of most to commit to attending the entire event. A group met regularly for Gospel Based Discipleship (see resource section) and Education For Ministry (EFM) was offered as it has been for over a decade. Sadly, much of this involved a relatively small cadre of people, many of them college educated and already open to self-disclosure and sharing. The majority of people were reluctant to be involved in much more than Sunday worship, and each church had its own specific issues. How to expand the involvement of others and enlarge the group of those committed to learning and growth was, and remains, a major issue for the Church in Micronesia.

One recent innovation has been to start conversation circles in the two churches most in need of re-visioning. Using material from Margaret Wheatley's book, *Turning to One Another*, groups meet regularly to talk over issues and together discern how to move forward. We are careful to insure that all get to speak, sometimes by talking to their neighbor first and then sharing with the whole group. This strategy, which is informal with less concern about structure and agenda, has great promise for helping people take responsibility for their churches and move forward in mission.

I am writing this in late summer of 2008. With less than six months of my time remaining, there is much left to do. A plan is emerging that will begin to tap the resources of assets in each congregation. The missioner on Saipan will likely divide her time between Guam and Saipan and will be the trained ordained leader for the mission. She is committed to implementing the Shared Ministry model she experienced in Wyoming and has the ability to cast a vision of what that could be like in the ECIM.

Other leaders are emerging and slowly taking on positions in their congregations that will develop as long as there is stable local support from the ECIM council and others. Two newly ordained deacons will assist the ministry on Guam, and a team of ordained and non-ordained leaders is being formed. The promise of continued partnership with the dioceses of Hawaii and Wyoming will keep ECIM from feeling so isolated and provide fresh ideas and opportunities for growth.

As we prepare to return to our home in West Missouri, Jane and I realize how blessed we are to have had two remarkable opportunities to assist the church in times of transition. I have learned that being a non-anxious presence can help others much more than being a fixer. People have shown me that not every problem has my name on it, and that it is a much better strategy to create structures for people to resolve their own issues. Conversation—informed by Scripture and prayer in an atmosphere of calm expectation—can open new opportunities even when people are experiencing personal loss and pining for what will never be again.

Chapter 10

A STORY OF INTENTIONAL INTERIM WORK IN THE UNITED CHURCH OF CHRIST

INEKE MITCHELL

One of the most exciting and challenging systems to traverse has to be transitional ministry in the United Church of Christ. In a denomination that is fifty years old with roots as deep and far away as the sixteenth century, tending to the interim process and inviting people of faith to tackle the developmental tasks is no small adventure. Add to that mix the variety of theological and liturgical traditions that have melded together from the Evangelical, Reformed, Congregational, and Christian streams, and you have a motley crew that can make your head spin. And, of course, the more recent influx of people of varying denominational backgrounds, many from Roman Catholic stock, responding to our invitation, "no matter who you are or where you are on life's journey you are welcome here," brings energy and life, but also its very own unique challenges.

Many of our congregations that are growing have welcomed "recovering Christians" from all sorts of authoritarian systems in addition to those who have never experienced church before, truly a wonderful and challenging adventure for all involved. And it doesn't quite stop there. There are still the geographic characteristics that influence the life of the community in ways over and above the denomination's many and varied traditions. My movement from the South to New England with stopovers in the Midwest and the Northwest has been an eye-opening journey. Serving as interim pastor and consultant, as trainer for the Interim Ministry Network (IMN), and more recently in a middle judicatory role has truly been, and still is, a privilege.

121

UCC polity is another interesting phenomenon to ponder. A respected theologian once said about his beloved denomination: "UCCers are Presbyterians who have trouble with authority." What he referred to was the tendency of congregations to lay claim to their congregational autonomy and relegate to the back burner the central tenet of our denominational life, namely, our covenantal relationships. The intentional interim pastor will do well by staying attuned to that reality and remembering that the two most important developmental tasks therefore become renewing denominational connections and coming to terms with history. And from the vantage point of my current judicatory role, I applaud and celebrate those who keep close contact and actively engage me in their process.

Someone might ask why in the world I would identify renewing denominational connections as so crucial to faithful and successful transitional work for an interim in the UCC. My answer is best relayed through two stories. The first story is the one of my own entry into interim ministry.

Balancing two careers and vocations in one household at times is a challenge. Mine arrived when it became my husband's turn to accept a promotion and exciting possibilities for expanding his professional development. Well aware of the timelines of searching for a new call in ministry, I embarked on my journey to a new setting for ministry as quickly as I could. I scheduled an appointment with one of the judicatory staff where we planned to relocate. That visit was short and sweet. Very few openings were available at the time and interim work was out of the question—only in-state and trained interims need apply. As it turned out, after actually relocating to the area I spent time doing vital ministry outside of the church which would not have been possible had I been able to engage in interim ministry.

Before a settled call could even be contemplated, let alone having all paperwork ready to go that route, we were on our way again to another state—my husband's job had been relocated again. This time I did not schedule an appointment with a judicatory official. "Casing the joint" first seemed a far better approach, being someone who does not enjoy outright rejection as a steady diet. I did, however, accept an invitation to come to the association's clergy gathering to meet some colleagues. This invitation was extended by the pastor of the congregation where we worshiped our first Sunday in our new community. Coincidentally, the judicatory official for the area participated in the clergy conversation. Over lunch we chatted and he asked if I was interested in serving as an interim. To make a long story short, I interviewed the following week and began my first interim call three weeks later.

Without any training in interim ministry and not knowing anything about the congregation or my new geographic setting and history, I realized very quickly that I would not be able to work effectively without a support system that could help me traverse this new ministry setting. The support of my colleagues was critical to a successful interim ministry.

Equally important was the congregation's willingness to engage in a type of ministry that was new to both of us. Indeed, without church leaders anxious to recapture the ministry to which they were called by graciously displaying faith and trust in my skills, being open to creativity and willing to explore all possibilities, reclaiming their identity and health would not have been possible. It is only with 20/20 hindsight that I still marvel at the power and presence of the Holy Spirit that enabled this ministry to be both faithful and successful. I am gratefully aware that it was through the resilience of a faithful community of believers, unwilling to give up and give in to their depression and grief after a painful and unhealthy departure of a long-loved pastor, that the transitional work of the congregation was possible.

The second story comes from my passion for scuba diving. After numerous visits to the coral reef, it has become one of my favorite metaphors for congregational life. It brings a refreshing addition to the marvelous metaphor of biblical proportions I also deem essential to successful transitional ministry: the Pauline gift of describing the faithful as the Body of Christ.

Scuba diving, at least as a recreational sport, should never be done alone. It demands training, practice, and unfailing trust in one's buddy. It also requires buoyancy control and a keen awareness of one's surroundings. In addition, it is essential to develop an ability to communicate clearly in creative ways and to commit to a willingness to adapt to the changing currents that might abruptly call for a change in travel direction. This also resembles the leadership style I prefer when working with congregations.

Congregational analysis can be helped by remembering the awesome experiences of traversing a coral reef. The ability to see life in seemingly dead places requires patience and a willingness to hang back and focus. The ability to recognize feeding frenzies for what they are, busy-ness and chaos parading as glorious activity, will help tremendously when entering into new and unfamiliar systems. This requires a willingness to ask tough questions and look beyond face value. Most of all, watching life and beauty of a thriving coral reef affirms in numerous ways the true interdependence necessary for a healthy system.

As a denomination, the United Church of Christ exists first and foremost for the local church. Each congregation is unique and autonomous in its decision-making. Our life together, however, resourcing and supporting one another similar to life on a reef, demands attention to our covenant and affirming that the whole is greater than the sum of its parts. The health and welfare of each local congregation is enriched by our life together, striving to answer Jesus' mandate "That All May Be One."

After several interim experiences and once again anticipating a move to a new location as a "trailing spouse," I decided it was time to be formally trained as an interim. Not knowing where we would land and what kind of requirements my new conference or association would have regarding interim ministry, it seemed the prudent road to travel. Training brought me new resources and skills and affirmed my intuitive gifts for this unique form of ministry. It offered an additional support system and, after joining the Interim Ministry Network faculty, it became a way to keep my skills honed and my knowledge updated, while allowing me to engage colleagues in learning together. And then, when the opportunity arose to put my experience and skills to work in yet another expression of ministry, I accepted with the excited anticipation that new adventures bring. I became an interim middle judicatory, which offered me the opportunity to engage in ministry looking through a new lens.

One of the very first engagements in my new role involved an opportunity to impress upon a group of lay leaders the importance and necessity of good interim work by a trained practitioner. One of the congregations in my care was in pain. The new, energetic, young pastor in a first full-time call ran headlong into a wall created by a congregation that had not taken the time to grieve the retirement of their long-term beloved pastor. They began their search for a new pastor immediately and during their interim time used a few retired pastors for worship leadership and pastoral care. The search committee had a difficult task and received little help from the congregation as they prepared their profile. As a result, the profile reflected the dreams and wishes of a few and spoke more about who they wanted to be, rather than who they were.

They were excited about calling a young and energetic pastor, and there was a brief surge of energy that lifted them out of their depression. It was not long, though, before the inexperience and idealism of someone new in ministry, who took at face value the dreams for ministry expressed in the church's profile during their search, collided with the grieving people afraid of all the new things that replaced the old and familiar. Unhealthy behavior resulted in secret meetings to petition the congregation for the immediate departure of the new pastor. A hurting, confused, dream-crushed, and faithful, yet sometimes bungling, pastor mustered enough grace to resign before too much damage was done to the congregation.

The end result of this unfortunate episode was the introduction of intentional interim ministry to the congregation. Through the telling of some of my own stories as an intentional interim, the congregational leaders allowed themselves to see me as a resource rather than a suspicious judicatory official. In almost all instances where I was able to share the benefits and opportunities of doing intentional interim work, the response was enthusiastic and open. It was not unusual to see and hear amazement and disappointment at never having heard this information before.

The gift of a denominational system such as ours can also become a frustration at times. Because of local church autonomy, one of the greatest challenges for judicatory staff is to discover ways to build relationships with congregational leaders before crises arrive. This is why I believe that the task of renewing denominational linkages is essential. As judicatory staff, honoring our polity means waiting to be invited into the life of a congregation. Unfortunately, this often happens very late and precludes the opportunity for preventive work. The story just told is a perfect example of why this task is so important. When teamwork happens and the covenant between congregation, interim pastor, and judicatory staff is allowed to flourish, miracles happen, ministry continues, and lives are changed. One example of a serendipitous encounter may be helpful.

A local church leader who is a lifelong UCCer attended a workshop where she, for the first time, discovered the availability of judicatory staff as a resource to the congregation. The pastor of her congregation was active in association work but had never really encouraged his laypeople to become active in wider church activities, even to the point of discouraging laity from attending association and conference meetings by stating "I'm going so I can be a delegate." In UCC polity that is very unfortunate but not unusual. Many local churches are not aware of the importance of their participation in the wider community. It still amazes me how many congregants have no clue about the availability and variety of resources created by the denomination for local congregations. This lay leader, however, was intrigued and contacted me as her regional minister. She was thrilled to discover the resources available. She also insisted that the pastor invite me to come and preach, which he did.

Not too long afterward, her pastor notified me of his intention to resign because he had accepted another call. Because I had already begun to develop a relationship with one of the congregation's lay leaders, I was able to become part of the process to prepare for the transition at a wonderfully early moment. These events unfolded the week before I was scheduled to preach. Consequently, I was able to be present in the congregation as the pastor delivered the news and then meet with members that day to offer my support and explain my role as their transition consultant. This became a wonderful opportunity to teach about our polity and to establish a partnership in ministry where members felt free to call on me often.

Engaged, caring, and committed intentional interim pastors in the United Church of Christ have recognized the importance of interdependence. The Interim Ministry Network has been a wonderful vehicle for making connections and resourcing one another. Important steps have been taken to spread the word and invite accountability. A support group that is truly "awesome" (Association of United Church of Christ Intentional Interim Ministers, with the acronym AUCCIIM) has grown into a superb network for those who feel called to this unique ministry. Because our denomination is what it is, this outgrowth of denominational caucus work at the IMN annual meeting is a place for me as a judicatory staff member to stay connected to practitioners in the field. AUCCIIM's leadership has developed wonderful tools such as easily downloadable flyers to be shared with congregations while also allowing their members to post their availability for service on their website. Check it out for yourself at www.aucciim.org.

All of what I've said so far speaks to renewing denominational connections. But what of the second important developmental task I mentioned, coming to terms with history? Why this one? In my opinion, and from my experience while serving as an intentional interim, over and over it became clear that the work of the search committee would get stuck if honest reflection on the congregation's past was either hurried or not approached with integrity.

I remember being called into a struggling system while wearing my independent consultant's hat. The congregation's named issue was, as it often is, that their pastor of three years wasn't living up to expectations, and a small group of powerful people was actively sabotaging her ministry. Over the course of an intensive two-day workshop with this congregation, it was marvelous to watch the discovery of and willingness to name honestly the real issue to be tackled.

This was a congregation whose history included a merger some thirty years earlier of two very different groups who, at first glance, had done everything right. They had sold both buildings, built a new church, changed their name, and were off to new life together. They grew steadily and seemingly were a thriving community. In the end, however, what they named was that, in reality, there were actually *three* congregations living in the same space: the two original congregations, and a new congregation of people who had joined after the merger and therefore could not understand some of the seemingly silly complaints.

The pastor's leadership was focused on this third congregation. During the search process and as revealed in their local church profile, the identity they presented did not truly reflect the story of their life. Their new pastor trusted the story told during the search and took them at their word. Congregations one and two were increasingly feeling left out, and during the workshop they were able to claim the truth, *thirty years later*, that they never really did the emotional work of merging and becoming one. They committed themselves to finally doing the work and engaged someone to work with them on those issues. The pastor was able to stay, and together they promised to tackle the hard work that was to come.

The liberating power of understanding, or at least gaining insight into, one's past is in the opportunity it brings to change behavioral patterns we are otherwise destined to repeat. One congregation's story became vividly clear when a timeline, drawn on a roll of wallpaper, revealed a sixty-year pattern of calling pastors, all of whom managed to betray the trust of the congregation in some important way.

The first one literally betrayed a confidence and was quietly sent to ride off into the sunset by a powerful group of elders without telling others why. Some still mourned that loss. The pastors that followed varied in their betrayals from misconduct to incompetence. All, however, created a pattern so subtle that it took much courage to discover the end result: an unconscious script, followed repeatedly by search committees, that clergy are not to be trusted, so let's make sure we pick one who proves us right. Through storytelling, often while shedding lots of tears, this congregation was able to grieve and heal and move beyond blaming denomination staff for their unfortunate choices of the past and engage in a search process that finally broke the haunting pattern.

Maybe my favoring the two tasks mentioned as primary is colored by my current position as a judicatory person who spends a large amount of time serving as a resource for search committees. For me, being able to work together with an intentional interim, particularly during the time of preparation of the congregational profile, is a joy. Modeling the interdependent relationship of search committee, intentional interim, and judicatory staff as something that benefits the whole congregation is what I strive for. Helping congregations discern a truly great match for their vision of ministry and mission depends on their willingness to disclose their true identity to potential candidates. It surely is a privilege and honor to watch congregations tend to their work and share in the celebration of a new covenant when new pastors are installed. For me in my position this is a gift that hopefully will grow into the ability to be consulted sooner rather than later when issues arise, conflicts appear, or crises threaten to derail a congregation's ministry.

Chapter 11

BEING AN "AFTER PASTOR"

Barry Miller

Those of us who have dedicated much of our time, energy, and commitment to serving as transitional pastors are aware that some congregations seem to be more than normally "anxious" during the interim time. By its very nature, transition is often a period of confusion, anxiety, and uncertainty, affecting members of the congregations in which we serve in many different ways. Add a situation in which the former pastor may have engaged in sexual misconduct with either a staff member or a member of the congregation or when there has been an allegation of embezzlement or inappropriate use of the congregation's funds, and the levels of anxiety, confusion, and uncertainty are raised exponentially. In these situations the specialized ministry of an "after pastor" is needed. Associates in Education and Prevention in Pastoral Practice, Inc. (AEPPP) defines after pastor as clergy serving in congregations where a former religious leader engaged in unethical conduct.[1] However, misconduct by a former pastor is not the only situation in which such experts find themselves attempting to help a congregation to heal. I will discuss some of these other situations later on in this chapter.

A number of years ago, I was called to be the intentional interim pastor of a pastoral-size congregation located in a suburban community in the Northeast. By the time I received this particular call, I had served in ordained ministry for nearly thirty years, including service as a transitional pastor in five congregations. In spite of this experience, I had never served in an after pastor capacity and knew nothing about this ministry. Supposedly this would be a relatively "low maintenance" pastorate. I assured them that I would continue to serve until they were once again able to call a full-time rector. In my interviews with the congregation and also with both the judicatory staff and the interim consultant assigned to this congregation, no mention of the congregation's history or relationships with its previous pastors came up. Furthermore, because I knew nothing about the ministry of after pastor, I did not ask about such things. In this case my ignorance and failure to ask important questions became the driving factor that led to my learning more about after pastor ministry than I ever would have imagined.

About eight weeks after I began as their interim pastor, I found the behavior of some of the members of the congregation to be quite out of the ordinary in ways that were neither expected nor which I had experienced in other congregations. A few members even told me, in quite strong language, that I was never around when I was needed. I replied that not only did I keep regular office hours but also I was diligent in visiting homes and hospitals. Furthermore, I maintained a record of my time both in the office as well as the time I spent on pastoral visits. Again, I was also told quite strongly by these same vocal and critical members that they were not happy with my ministry. One of the critics presented me with a "laundry list" of my failings as their pastor. I knew that they had barely gotten to know me in such a short time. My "gut" instincts and the training in interim ministry led me to think perhaps there was something else going on that was contributing to this antagonism.

My wife, Nancy, is also a trained interim pastor. At the time I was dealing with the issues in the parish, she was serving as the deployment officer on the judicatory staff. I realized that she would be an excellent resource to help me address the situation. I explained to her that I thought the intensity with which I was being criticized, both to my face and in conversations related to me by other parishioners, seemed to be significantly out of proportion to what I was saying and doing. Nancy remarked that perhaps I needed to find out more about the congregation's history and its past clergy relationships. She suggested I get in touch with the interim consultant to see if some light could be shed on the situation. And so I did.

When I met with the consultant, I discovered that this congregation had a very "interesting" history, to say the least. Twenty years before I arrived, the rector had allegedly been involved in inappropriate sexual behavior with a number of the girls in the parish's Girl Scout troop. Some of the victims' parents were still active members of the congregation. In those days, clergy who were allegedly inappropriate were removed from the congregation, hopefully never again to be permitted to practice ministry in a parish. This particular pastor, indeed, was removed by the bishop. He relocated to another state where he began a career in another position not connected with ministry.

The next pastor was an interim who stayed for about fourteen months and whose ministry was uneventful. The parish then called a recovering alcoholic as rector who "fell off the wagon" shortly after arriving in the parish. It was stated that this priest often had to be awakened on Sunday mornings and sobered up by some parishioners before Sunday services could begin. Needless to say, this was not a happy time.

After a while the alcoholic priest took another position and moved away from the area. This pastorate was also followed by an uneventful period with an interim pastor who remained there for the usual time of a year or so. The parish next called a priest who was to experience a major trauma in the congregation's history: The church building was struck by lightning and burned to the ground. It was also during his time with them that he confessed to the congregation that he had been sexually molested as a child and was experiencing great difficulty both in his personal life and in his leadership of the congregation. Helping the congregation to cope with the demanding task of finding another place to worship had become a source of extraordinary stress. After the congregation engaged in bitter arguments about how they wanted to rebuild the church, the congregation split down the middle. A number of people left, not to return even when the rebuilding was completed. Lack of funds to support a full-time rector further complicated the situation. Faced with financial stress due to lower income, the rector looked for and found another position.

Following his departure, a priest-in-charge came to serve a three-year term on a part-time basis. The priest-in-charge is appointed by the bishop and sometimes is eligible to become the called pastor. This priest had retired from full-time active ministry and was able to provide worship services for the congregation. This was satisfactory since his hours were minimal and his compensation was not a particular burden to the congregation during this extended time of recovery from the devastating fire and the turmoil during the time of rebuilding. After the priest-in-charge completed his three-year obligation, I arrived on the scene.

When I realized I was in a situation that I was not equipped to handle, I reached out for help to my interim ministry clergy colleagues who informed me that the Interim Ministry Network was hosting a seminar and workshop to train people for "after pastor" ministry. This is when I discovered that after pastor ministry was the description of the situation where I was serving. Thankfully, the program offered me advice and training on how to cope with the issues so that neither I nor the members of the parish would inflict further damage on each other. It would also help us both to do the ministry we all wanted to accomplish there.

I am very grateful for the work that people like Nancy Myer Hopkins, Deborah Pope-Lance, and others have done in their lectures, workshops, and in literature describing the special ministry of serving congregations after an incident or incidents of clergy misconduct. Without them I believe we would have far more "failed" pastorates of clergy who follow clergy who had difficulty with boundary issues in their ministry. I am also grateful for the services of the clinical therapist who is retained by my diocese. He was instrumental in facilitating a general meeting with the members of the parish in order to open the conversation about the impact of the previous clergy misconduct and then helped design a process for healing. The congregation appears to be healthy and thriving under its new clergy leadership.

What exactly is "after pastor" ministry and what goes on in a congregation following misconduct by the clergy? Deborah Pope-Lance states that serving in the aftermath of a predecessor's misconduct often feels like being an Emergency Medical Responder at the scene of an accident.[2] Trained EMRs know that it is a mistake to try to attend to everything that is going on at the scene. Instead, they are taught that moving the physical debris of the accident or directing traffic is not the best way to aid the victims. Their first task, as an Emergency Medical Responder, is to attend to the needs of the injured. She goes on to say that clergy, following colleagues who have been inappropriate, should understand that they too, like the EMRs, cannot do everything and need to concentrate on the need to be a pastor, restoring trust in the office and person of minister to their congregation. It is inappropriate for an after pastor to be involved in any way with the judicatory tasks that need to be done in order to deal with the offender. If the after pastor sincerely wants the congregation to begin healing during the interim time, he or she should not publicly state an opinion of the offending clergy person or interact in any way with the media.

Nancy Myer Hopkins says that the identity of the "victim," the person who was the subject of the offending clergy person's boundary violation, should be kept as confidential as possible and only revealed to persons who have a need to know.[3] This, of course, would be the officers of the congregation as well as the judicatory officials who must deal with the alleged offender. However, Hopkins goes on to say that the congregation must be told as soon as feasible exactly what is alleged to have happened and what the consequences will be for the offender. Congregations where this disclosure is not made are subject to being negatively affected by the "secret" for many years. Their ability to be engaged in the work of mission and ministry for which the congregation exists is gravely compromised

Darlene Haskin has described some of the situations after pastors have experienced in serving a congregation following clergy misconduct.[4] One after pastor said that he remembered his struggle with being so mistrusted. He wondered what he had done to earn such deep suspicion by some of the members of the congregation. When he made efforts to provide honest communication, he was usually unheard, misheard, or his intentions were questioned. When he sought information about what had happened with the previous pastor, the parish leadership suddenly fell into a state of amnesia. He later learned that the previous pastor had left in a hurry with all kinds of rumors surrounding his departure. Time and the absence of the offending pastor are often not enough to heal betrayals of pastoral trust.

Another pastor told of being greeted as "our savior" by the congregation when he first arrived. His "honeymoon" was short and sweet, with the emphasis on "short." Soon he was accused of not doing anything. After a long struggle, he and the congregation's leadership finally arrived at a common understanding of realistic job expectations.

After pastors have found that in working in congregations in which the "secret" is kept, where there has been no attempt to shine light on the misconduct of previous clergy, many seemingly small issues turn into major crises and confrontations. Consultants and experts in the area of after pastor ministry state unless there is a public process to help the congregation toward its healing, the pressure on the after pastor to "fix" everything is increased. Even if there is a well-thought-out, well-designed process, the pressure on the after pastor can still be intense.

Haskin goes on to say that in the more difficult cases where the congregation refuses to admit that anything is wrong and denies that it needs any help, the after pastor often becomes the target for the rage and anger that the members of the congregation are unwilling or unable to admit exists.[5]

I found myself in a situation similar to those described above when I served another parish. In this case I served as a "severely uninformed or purposely misinformed" after pastor. This situation was one that I will remember clearly for a long time to come.

I began an interim position in a congregation about which I had been assured by the judicatory that everything was fine, except that the former rector's spouse was serving as the senior warden, the highest lay leadership position in an Episcopal parish. In my discussions with the judicatory I was assured that, although this was normally thought to be irregular, this particular clergy spouse was functioning quite effectively as senior warden. The junior warden headed the interim pastor's search committee and was my significant contact person during the time I was interviewing for the position.[6] I was once again assured, this time by the junior warden, that things were working out very well with the former rector's spouse holding that particular office. He assured me that no one in the parish or at the judicatory thought that this was problematic.

Before I began as the interim pastor, the bishop of the diocese appointed a pastor, who was unemployed at the time, to act as priest-in-charge of this congregation for a three-year term. The letter of agreement, signed by the cleric and affirmed by the senior warden and the bishop of the diocese, gave the cleric the option to be called by the congregation as its settled pastor. Before he completed the three-year assignment, this priest instead accepted a call to serve another congregation in a diocese located some distance away. Knowing all this history of irregular governance, I still accepted the call as interim. Certainly I entertained some reservations about the parish, but went there anyhow. I started this new assignment on April 1; April Fool's Day—how ironic!

Shortly after I began my ministry in this congregation, a few parishioners told me that they strongly suspected that the senior warden was having an affair with the former priest-in-charge and that one reason he left was because the situation was beginning to become more publicly known. Others came to me with the same story, at which point I realized that it would be necessary to get some professional advice as to how to proceed with handling this information.

During the previous five years when I had served in a parish that had experienced multiple crises, I was fortunate to have been in a supervised after pastor support group sponsored by the local judicatory. Our supervisor, a clinical therapist, was also ordained. He was most helpful to us as we dealt with the "psychological debris" in our congregations resulting from the misconduct of the previous pastor or pastors. One of the clergy in the group was also trained as a therapist and had done many assignments as an after pastor. He was also connected with a national organization that dealt with issues of clergy misconduct and was an instructor in the diocese's "Safe Church" certification programs for clergy and for laypersons serving in youth ministry and Christian education in their parishes. These people, who understood the kind of problems I was encountering, were and continued to be very important in supporting my ministry.

When I called the supervisor and told him what I had uncovered, I asked him what he thought I needed to do. He responded by asking me, "What do you think you need to do?" I replied that I thought the first thing was to get in touch with the bishop as soon as possible. He confirmed that was exactly what needed to be done, and emphasized that it should be done immediately.

I should point out here that the interim pastor has a special relationship with the bishop. In the polity of the Episcopal Church, when there is not a settled rector, the legal reality is that the bishop serves as rector. The interim then acts on behalf of the bishop. Therefore, it is important that the interim pastor have a close relationship with the bishop or a judicatory official designated by the bishop.

When I saw the bishop a few days later, he seemed to be very supportive. He told me that I should meet with the senior warden to let her know the information brought to me by these parishioners. He and I agreed that it would be best if she would resign from or temporarily step down from the warden's position.

When I later met with the senior warden, she strongly denied the allegations and refused to leave her position. The following day the junior warden stormed into my office, stating that I should have come to him first before I went to the bishop and that he, as junior warden, would have told me that there was no truth to the allegations.

The junior warden's strong and surprising reaction may have had to do with his own history, which I learned later. The junior warden was in his fourth marriage and his current wife was formerly married to another priest in the area with whom she allegedly had an affair while both were still married to their previous spouses. No wonder he was protective of the senior warden! The junior warden said that he and the senior warden had already spoken to the bishop and that they were going to meet with him. He also informed me that I was not going to attend that meeting. I wondered if he was identifying with his own past misconduct.

Things went downhill from there rapidly. Unfortunately for me, the bishop agreed with the wardens that I should leave the parish immediately. It was painfully obvious to me that I would not receive the judicatory support that might have been helpful to both the parish and to me. A short time later, I also learned that this congregation had a long history of clergy or clergy spouses who had problems with alcohol abuse.

I refused to resign my position and told the wardens that if they wanted to fire me, it was their prerogative to do so, as long as the terms of the letter of agreement we signed would be upheld. Obviously, this whole situation came to a very unhappy conclusion. The members of the parish were informed by a very brief letter announcing that I would no longer be serving as interim pastor.

There was no further explanation from the wardens to the congregation. I received phone calls, asking me to explain what happened, which I referred back to the wardens for further information. Some parishioners asked me if I had I done something illegal or immoral. I let them know that it certainly was not the issue. I can only assume that there were others in the congregation who also thought I was guilty of some impropriety.

In sorting out this confusing and stressful situation, I found helpful insight from E. Larraine Frampton:

> If the After Pastor enters the scene when the level of conflict is high, ground rules for communications, behavior, process, and contracts should be in place before the ministry begins. The After Pastor will need as much support and as many resources as the judicatory can provide.
>
> When the After Pastor has been in the community for a relatively short time, factions in the congregations might lift up the "sins" of the After Pastor to judicatory leaders, plead that he or she should be removed. The challenge for the judicatory is to resist being triangulated against the After Pastor and for the factions. This is not the moment to conduct a pastoral performance review, even if congregations request it. My experience has been that congregations use pastoral performance reviews at this time to prove that the After Pastor is ineffective and should be removed.
>
> The judicatory leaders may have some power or leverage at this juncture in the congregation's life, because they are the ones who appoint or recommend potential clergy for the congregation. They can use that leverage to encourage members to support outside consultants, who can stabilize the system and provide a process to address the real issues, rather than the personality of the After Pastor. The judicatory may refuse to recommend candidates until the congregation has completed the process. . . .
>
> When disclosure is greatly delayed or there is no disclosure, pastors who follow the offender often experience conflict

with the congregation for years to come. Unresolved anger or distrust of each successive clergyperson is acted out in indirect and subversive ways. Leaders will find a pattern of short-term clergy with three- to six-year terms.[7]

Frampton goes on to state that this kind of conflict experience exhibits a variety of symptoms, including

- Closed communication system;

- Weak personal boundaries;

- Decision-making processes that are not functioning;

- Various levels of knowledge about the misconduct, as well as all of the other dynamics often found in a congregation where there has been abuse by clergy.

Sometimes even the best models for dealing with conflicted congregations fail to work and the congregation continues to be reactive.

In the situation described above, the judicatory lacked an understanding of the processes described by Frampton. While many who are well informed of the need to support after pastors in their ministry and do so with a strong sense of commitment, there is an ongoing need for more education. Perhaps one day all judicatory officials will understand the difficulties after pastors face and how isolated and hopeless the after pastors may feel without appropriate understanding or support from their judicatories.

In preparation for writing this chapter, I spoke with several colleagues who are experienced after pastors. Their stories give an indication of some of the situations faced by after pastors. Bob (not his real name of course), a colleague of mine with long experience in after pastor ministry, related some of his "war stories" to me. I think some of his observations are worth including here.[8]

Bob commented that most people tend to associate this very special type of transitional ministry with misconduct and its consequences. It is, of course, true that trained after pastors can be and, arguably, should be used in these most difficult situations because of their special skills and experience. Bob went on to say that he has learned that the after pastor can be and indeed should be used in a broader situational range. He believes that this ministry is effective in any situation in which there has been an unexpected or unplanned severing of a pastoral relationship between a clergyperson and a congregation. This can occur even in situations that may have nothing to do with misconduct but which, nonetheless, cause the same trauma and congregational dynamics. I would add that the services of an after pastor can be helpful following any traumatic change.

Bob's first after pastor assignment came at a time in the church long before we used this term and had nothing to do with clergy misconduct. A young, dynamic, and popular priest died quite unexpectedly in his office. Within 48 hours of the death of this beloved young priest, Bob was asked by the bishop to serve as the interim. When he walked into the congregation, he discovered that they were in profound shock and struggling with the first stages of grief. It was in every sense an after pastor assignment. He worked with the wardens, vestry, staff, and the entire congregation to try to make sense of what appeared to make no sense. This diocese provided several excellent resource people who were experts in dealing with grieving in individuals and communities. The situation was further complicated by the fact that the dead priest's wife was also ordained and was a member of the congregation's staff. He described this experience as one of the most challenging after-pastor situation he has encountered in his years in ministry.

In another situation, in yet another diocese, Bob was asked to work with a congregation that had come to the painful conclusion that they had not made a good match in calling their new rector. This priest, who had arrived just a few months earlier, concurred with this conclusion. It had become obvious to the priest and to the congregation that things were not "as advertised" on either side of the equation. The priest knew that finding another call was the only option for his well-being and that of the congregation. The level of guilt and responsibility for what had clearly been a mistaken match lived on for many months. There were recriminations directed at both the search committee and the vestry, not to mention the anger projected onto the bishop.

Bob summarized his stories by saying that the cases of misconduct he has experienced have been varied and have not always involved sexual impropriety, but the impact on the congregation is always profound, extensive, and long-lasting.

Another colleague, whom we shall identify as Jim—not his real name—also related some of his experiences as an after pastor to me.

Jim served as an intentional interim pastor in a number of situations since the early 1990s, some of which have turned out to involve clergy who have engaged in inappropriate sexual behavior with members of their congregations. There were some common issues, but each case was unique in the circumstances of the offending clergyperson. Jim recounted that there often was a high level of distrust of the clergy who followed in the wake of previous clergy misconduct. Members of the congregation were often angry with each other and with the clergy who served them in the wake of the previous misbehavior of others.

Jim told how his first encounter with an after pastor congregation was during the time he was employed by a faith-based company in the early 1990s. The CEO was also the former pastor of the congregation where Jim was now serving on a part-time basis. To further complicate matters, the CEO's wife was also the receptionist at the society's offices. One day she received a call in which she was informed that she had left her luggage in a hotel room in Florida. She was quite confused, since she had not been traveling in Florida. When she realized her husband had made the trip, supposedly by himself, she confronted him and asked him who the woman was who left luggage in his hotel room. He confessed that he was having an affair with one of the members of his former congregation and that the woman had given birth to his son. Upon receiving this news, she asked him to leave. The company also dismissed him as CEO. He and his wife divorced and he later married the other woman. The other woman remained married to him for a while, but later left him after she had an affair with someone else. Further, Jim learned that it was alleged that the pastor/CEO departed from his first church over an issue of sexual misconduct.

Can you imagine how Jim felt, trying to sort out this messy situation of scandal on top of scandal, with his boss as the perpetrator? Fortunately for both Jim and the congregation, Jim learned about after pastor ministry and got some training. With the aid of a mentor, Jim was able to keep his head straight when accusations started to fly. His ability to maintain a stable, non-reactive presence and to trust in himself when no one else did helped keep things from getting worse. However, the congregation has continued to decline and has experienced problems in keeping pastors longer than just a year or two. Problems of this magnitude are not easily solved. Poor stewardship—a symptom of lack of trust of clergy who follow after misconduct—continues to be a problem. Jim believes that things will not get better until the congregation is ready to deal with the real problem and demonstrates this commitment by calling a full-time after pastor.

Another of Jim's stories involved a church with a messy history of staff sexual misconduct, which was exacerbated by the congregation's predilection for making choices based on popularity. When finances got tight, the church had to cut the paid staff. They chose to retain the popular director of Christian education, who had a history of misconduct, and terminated the pastor. Some time later Jim came in as after pastor. He had to lead them through the difficult process of realizing they had made choices based on popularity, not on the spiritual needs of the congregation. Once he gained some trust, Jim was able to help them to reprioritize their values.

These are but a few of the many experiences after pastors have encountered in doing intentional interim ministry. When I think about my own experience and those of others, I come to a few key points to share:

- Full advance disclosure—this means before the after pastor arrives;

- The value of a mentor;

- Training in the work of the after pastor;

- A colleague support group;

- Relationship of mutual trust with the judicatory;

- Good self-care;

- Appropriate awareness of one's own issues and limitations.

I hope that the stories I have shared are convincing testimony to the value of each of these points. After pastor ministry is not for everyone. It is not needed in the majority of situations, but when called for, it truly is a gift from God.

Those of us who have invested in education and training in this highly specialized calling feel that if we can make a difference in helping to bring about healing in the wounded congregations we serve, we are, in fact, doing God's work. After pastors are steadfast in the belief that this ministry is one that can hasten reconciliation and help to bring about the healing needed by the congregation before the next pastor is called.

Notes

1. http://www.aeppp.org/afterpastor.htm

2. Deborah Pope-Lance, "Afterpastors: Restoring Pastoral Trust," in *When a Congregation Is Betrayed: Responding to Clergy Misconduct,* ed. Beth Ann Gaede (Herndon, VA: Alban Institute, 2006), 53.

3. Nancy Myer Hopkins, "Best Practices After Betrayal Is Discovered," *When a Congregation Is Betrayed: Responding to Clergy Misconduct,* 2.

4. Darlene K. Haskin, "After Pastors in Troubled Congregations," in *Restoring the Soul of a Church: Healing Congregations Wounded by Clergy Sexual Misconduct,* ed. Nancy Myer Hopkins and Mark Laaser (Collegeville, MN: Liturgical Press, 1995), 155.

5. Ibid.

6. Junior warden is the title given to the second-highest lay office in congregations in the Episcopal Church.

7. E. Larraine Frampton, "Conflict Management: Selecting the Right Tools," *When a Congregation is Betrayed: Responding to Clergy Misconduct,* 34.

8. These accounts of experiences in after pastor interim ministry are

used with permission of the clergy who forwarded them for my use in this chapter. Their names have not been revealed in order to protect their anonymity.

Chapter 12

THE BEST-KEPT SECRET IN THE LUTHERAN CHURCH

Lawrence L. Hand

One of the best-kept secrets in Protestantism is that the patriarch of the Lutheran Church just might be the first unofficial interim pastor to serve in North America. Lutheranism was brought to America in the early eighteenth century by groups of immigrants from Germany. These faithful people were accustomed to the state church system in their homeland but were at a loss in their new world settlements, suffering from a serious deficit of structure and leadership.

In 1742, as an answer to their cry for help, 31-year-old Henry Melchior Muhlenberg was sent from the homeland to minister to the Lutherans in three Pennsylvania congregations. Muhlenberg was blessed with energetic leadership ability, common sense, and could preach in English, German, and Dutch. Upon arrival, he discovered that the three congregations he was called to serve were widely scattered across eastern Pennsylvania, requiring hundreds of miles of travel by horseback each week. Two of the congregations had been taken over by young impostors pretending to be credentialed ministers. Muhlenberg quickly got rid of the imposters and trained lay leaders who would serve in his absence. All the while his clarion call to the people was *"Ecclesia Plantada"* or *"The Church must be planted."* In subsequent years of ministry, he traveled on missionary trips to surrounding states, gathering and organizing the scattered Lutherans into congregations. Churches and schoolhouses were built and provided with leadership. He was a skilled arbitrator in church arguments, restoring order where needed. After six years of masterful leadership, Muhlenberg called together a synod of pastors and representative laymen from each parish. It was time to bring unity to all the churches he served by organizing them into a representative church body endowed with the power to license and install their own ministers and to govern themselves independently from the state church in Germany. Thus the seeds for the Lutheran Church in America were sown and the Ministerium of Pennsylvania, which today is known as the Southeastern Pennsylvania Synod of the Evangelical Lutheran Church in America, was formed.

Henry Muhlenberg, the patriarch of Lutheranism in the new world, was in effect the first "interim pastor" to serve the Lutheran Church. He was called as a missionary to the new world to serve those who made the courageous decision to "transition" from the old world to the new. Their faith came with them, but they needed a leader like Muhlenberg to help them rediscover their mission as the people of God in a new world and culture. The itinerant style of his ministry was his legacy and is carried on in the itinerant movement from one placement to the next of our interim pastors today. He managed shifts in leadership, kept his congregations connected to the larger church and helped them establish their identity, and brought clarity of God's mission for them in that place. The people rediscovered their purpose as the Body of Christ and the church was planted in the heart of their emerging communities. The church of the old world was transformed into the church of the new world and maintained relevancy at the center of its new life and culture.[1]

Henry Muhlenberg was laid to rest on October 7, 1787, in "preacher's row" in the graveyard of Augustus Lutheran Church in Trappe, Pennsylvania, not far from the original church building that he erected, which still stands as the oldest unaltered Lutheran Church in America. Since the time Muhlenberg stepped foot on these shores, the Lutheran Church, like many mainline denominations, has remained unaltered like the church he first built. We have enjoyed our common approach to being the church and have relished a comfortable place at the center of the lives of the faithful and the communities where they live.

> The great obstacle to discovering the shape of
> the earth, the continents, and the ocean was not
> ignorance but the illusion of knowledge.[2]

Since the early 1960s our society and culture, locally and globally, has undergone a dramatic upheaval. This "new world" has become confusing and anxious spiritually, politically, and psychologically. The spiritual, moral, and functional foundations of our church have slowly been overgrown by a plethora of scattered values and ideals. We have been pushed to the fringe of our culture, yet we have fought to remain unchanged through enormous cultural shifts. We have taken shelter in the "illusion of knowledge" that the church remains at the center of our new world in the same way the religious and secular authorities of the Middle Ages, despite evidence to the contrary, refused to believe that the earth was round and that the earth orbited the sun. The greatest obstacle standing in the way of a new "reformation" and newly discovered ways to be the church is the continuing illusion that the church we have maintained for centuries remains relevant to our culture. The hard truth is that we are not. Early in 2008, the Pew Research Center released the results of a study that clearly challenges any illusions that we can continue to be the same church we have been for the past 250 years. The data convincingly revealed that fewer people are members of any churches, fewer people are going to church, more people claim to be nonreligious, only 18 percent of U.S. residents are mainline Christians, and only one-third of people who are mainline Christians go to church regularly.[3] In my experience, people still claim to believe in God but the majority of those same disillusioned individuals have disassociated themselves from their church locally and denominationally.

I believe that many of the problems and conflicts encountered in declining mainline congregations directly relate to the inability to let go of our illusion and accept the reality that the church cannot be what it has always been in this new world and culture. Church leaders instead are being called forth to be ambassadors for Christ (2 Corinthians 5:16–21), sojourners in a foreign land. Like Muhlenberg and the congregations he planted, our faith communities face the challenge of being "mission outposts" to the frontier of the twenty-first century.

As ambassadors for Christ, the ELCA in southeastern Pennsylvania has been reclaiming our missional heritage and imagination. In 1994, 252 years after Muhlenberg set foot on the territory known today as the Southeastern Pennsylvania Synod, Bishop Roy Almquist was elected, by that very same judicatory, to his first term in office.

The challenges facing any new bishop are overwhelming, but when a parish pastor is elected bishop—as opposed to someone coming from a position in the larger church—the learning curve is even more daunting. In particular, he discovered that current practice in settled pastoral transitions was not serving our long-term missional needs. Congregations would be assigned a vice pastor who often was a neighboring Lutheran pastor who checked in with the leadership occasionally for visitation and emergency needs. The congregation was labeled "vacant" and marched in place until a new pastor arrived. Mission and ministry had its own momentum and delivery system. Membership and financial needs were met without much need for planning. Evangelism required minimal effort because members were born into families that were already part of the congregation. Society was much less mobile than today. If families relocated, they sought out membership in the local congregation on their own. This worked well during the decades leading up to the early 1960s when the church was pushed more to the fringe.

Marching in place often led to the choice of the same type of pastor as the predecessor. Mission and ministry became less effective and relevant. In short, congregations did not see the time of transition as a ripe opportunity to separate spiritually and emotionally from their former pastor. They rarely used the time to heal and resolve issues and conflicts that might undercut and sabotage future mission and ministry. Above all, they were not engaging in any intentional process of discerning God's mission for their future. Congregational leadership focused their energy on forming the call committee post-haste in order to "get" a new pastor in place. This search-and-hire model had little room for prayerful and intentional discernment of mission and blurred how God was working through them to "call" their next pastor. Much of the push for the immediate call of a new settled pastor came from a collective fear that membership would drop off, financial contributions would decline, and worship attendance would suffer.

As their fears became reality, many congregations found themselves "at risk"[4] and living in fear for their survival. The urgency to call the next pastor was heightened and hastily made decisions often resulted in poor or inadequate matches. The quick-fix approach often led to unrealized mission and ministry potential and, in many cases, outright conflict. While many congregations were at a loss for new and creative ways to engage in mission, their anxiety and fear often fueled creative ways to be in conflict and a new search process for someone to blame. In some instances, the pastor would be accused of inadequacy. In many other cases, the synod was blamed for sending them the pastor even though in Lutheran polity, the call to a pastor comes from the congregation.

One incident that clearly demonstrates what we were encountering with congregations in transition was a meeting that the bishop and I were asked to attend to discuss the upcoming transition process. The previous pastorate had ended poorly. Their small city neighborhood had changed dramatically and the congregation was in a slow and steady decline. The leadership made it clear that they wanted to call their next settled pastor immediately. We requested a closed meeting with the church council so as to discuss our reasons for wanting them to work with a trained interim pastor and to focus their energy on discerning their mission and the appropriate pastor to lead them. When we arrived for the meeting and were ushered into a church parlor, there was much tension in the air. The parlor doubled as a meeting space and classroom, with an old vinyl accordion door that was drawn closed in order to give our meeting privacy. At least, that was what we thought. The council president who had assured us ahead of time that the meeting would be a closed session informed us in his opening statement that there were members of the congregation who were demanding to take part in our meeting. When we reminded them that an open meeting would not be appropriate at this time, he nodded his head as a signal to two other council members waiting by the accordion door. The doors were rolled away and quietly seated behind the accordion door, waiting in ambush, was a large group of members who proceeded to shout at us, angrily hurling accusations and insults. They blamed the synod for the failure of the former pastorate and their state of decline. They demanded their next pastor immediately so as to salvage a dying congregation. It was not one of our finer moments in middle judicatory service. This "ecclesiastical road rage" was a direct sign that something very deep and serious was going wrong in our congregational systems.

The fascinating history of this congregation is that one-and-a-half centuries ago the missional imagination of these English-speaking Lutherans led them to make the bold decision to break apart from their German-speaking counterparts in their sister congregation that was planted by and under the care of Muhlenberg. God was calling them to form an English-speaking congregation that would be more relevant to their changing community and culture. Over time, however, their missional heritage and imagination were lost. Once courageously venturing forth to do a new thing, they were now in steady decline, collapsing into a mode of survival that was suffocating them to death.

In the mid-1990s we were faced with the difficult challenge of providing resources to congregations that would empower them to recapture their missional heritage and imagination. It was also clear that a new, more relevant way of being the church could not be forced on congregations. As any good systems thinker knows, organizations will not be receptive to your attempt to offer help unless they are moving in your direction emotionally and spiritually. It became clear to our synodical leadership that the time of transition was exactly the time when congregations move in the direction of the middle judicatory. For that reason we made a primary strategic decision to focus our energies on improving the ways in which we assist congregations at this critical time in their life.

In 1999, the synod council of the Southeastern Pennsylvania Synod, at Bishop Almquist's recommendation, extended a call for me to serve as an assistant to the bishop. One of my key responsibilities would be to develop an effective network of intentional interim pastors and a structure that would provide ministry resources to congregations in transition. At the time there was an eclectic cadre of transitional pastors involved in this ministry who decided to gather periodically for support and learning. Some were on leave from call for graduate work, some were on leave from call because their settled ministry had ended poorly, and others sensed a call to this type of ministry long-term but admittedly lacked sufficient skills. Only one retired pastor was trained specifically for this type of ministry.

The first decision we made as synod staff was to commit ourselves to using trained intentional interim pastors in every viable transitional congregation. Congregations below the "at-risk" level that were dying required ministry in the form of hospice care. The second was to bring structure and consistency to the transition process. A pastoral transition manual was developed for interim pastors and congregational leaders detailing the phases of the process. To further the need for consistency in our praxis, every person serving under the title of interim pastor was required to complete the training provided by the Interim Ministry Network (IMN).[5] We contracted with the IMN to provide a mass training for all our interim pastors and those in neighboring synods. Pastors currently serving as interims who did not want to commit to our standards and practices self-selected out of the evolving network. This left us with highly motivated and trained interim pastors for the newly forming network in our synod.

The manual and our approach to interim ministry were built around the "five developmental tasks"[6] of the interim process. The development of an effective interim network would be undergirded by the robust church missiological principles and best practices[7] for middle judicatories. The highest level of collegial accountability in our synod exists to this day within our network. We hold each other accountable to the standards for interim service found in the ELCA Guidelines for Interim Ministry[8] and the established IMN Standards for Interim Ministry.[9] At every quarterly network gathering of interim pastors, we learn together in a two-hour continuing education opportunity led by outside presenters, which is followed by an Integrated Learning Experience (ILE)[10] in which we support and challenge each other professionally.

In order to have an official call from the synod council, every interim pastor is required to go through an "endorsement process." The endorsement process recognizes two important realities that exist in every denomination when it comes to interim pastoral service. In our Lutheran polity these two realities are called "candidacy" and "mobility." Candidacy refers to the process of community discernment (also used for settled ministry) that evaluates the appropriateness of individuals for initial and ongoing interim ministry in the church. Mobility refers to the system and protocols in the Lutheran Church whereby rostered leaders move from one call to another. Appropriate placements for interim pastors in our synod are determined collaboratively by the bishop, synodical staff, the director of interim ministry, the dean of interim ministry, and the conference dean. The transitional needs of the congregation are assessed and aligned with the appropriate leadership style and skills of an available interim pastor. Prerequisites for endorsement are good standing on the roster of our synod; approval by our transition ministry development team; completion of mobility papers;[11] a meeting with the dean of interim ministry or the director of interim ministry; a structured interim mobility interview with a team of two leaders from our synod staff, deans, or transitional ministry team; references from former ministry situations; a certificate of completion of the IMN training; annual continuing education related to interim skill development; signing our interim ministry covenant for service; regular participation in all official gatherings of our network; regular quarterly written reports to synodical staff and deans; and a thorough evaluation of the interim process at the time of closure.

In order to increase support to interim pastors and congregations, the position of dean of interim ministry was added to the bylaws of our synodical constitution. The dean fully participates as an advisor to the bishop's office as part of the committee of deans. We have formed a transition ministry development team consisting of professional and lay leaders that have experienced an effective interim process in their congregation. The team oversees the endorsement process, supports the development of our interim network, and provides education about intentional interim ministry to our congregations and synodical leaders. In order to aid in their support of interim pastors, all conference deans and synodical staff are provided with an orientation to the work of transitional ministry. Because interim ministry was an emerging priority, the synod council was challenged to provide financial support in the budget. Financial aid is offered for IMN training of interim pastors and continuing education opportunities.

Working collaboratively with synod staff, conference deans, and the director and dean of interim ministry, we have developed protocols for the placing of our interim pastors. Each interim receives a place-specific call to a congregation extended by our synod council. Interim pastors hold the same roster status and receive compensation and benefits equivalent to that of the outgoing pastor.

When the interim process is initiated, the pastoral transition manual is provided to the exiting pastor and the council leadership. This review leads to questions and conversation between synod staff, deans, and church leadership. After an interim is recommended, the "joining" process begins with a meeting between the conference dean, the bishop's assistant, and the executive officers of the congregation. In the next step, the interim pastor meets with the whole church council. Details of the transitional process, ongoing support from the bishop's office, and compensation are discussed at each level of the joining process. An exit interview between the exiting pastor and the council is facilitated by the synod staff and conference dean. This interview provides helpful guidance to the transition process to follow. The interim pastor and congregation enter into a letter of agreement and the start date is established. When a trained interim pastor is not immediately available, we provide a "bridge pastor" to serve for a period of one to three months. Bridge pastors receive the first phase of the IMN training and are full participants in our interim network. We also deploy bridge pastors after the long-term interim is reassigned. They serve until the completion of the call process.

Our network has also encouraged the use of potential and trained interim pastors from outside of our synod and denomination. Several of our interim pastors have served in non-Lutheran settings quite successfully. Our former bishop, upon completing the IMN training, recently completed an interim placement in an Episcopal parish in the neighboring diocese. The full-communion partnership between the Lutheran Church and other denominations has made orderly exchange possible for settled and interim service. Persons seeking interim mobility from inside and outside of our synod are given the opportunity to seek endorsement as prescribed above.

What began as an eclectic group of interim pastors has grown into one of the most influential and effective interim networks in North America. It truly has been a reformation in our approach to interim ministry. Through the commitment of synodical leadership and interim pastors, we are convinced that intentional interim ministry makes a difference in the long-term health of our congregations and the larger church. Trained intentional interim pastors, together with congregational leaders, have truly captured the spirit of what it means to be ambassadors for Christ. This important ministry has led us back into our new world. Communities of faith are better able to bear witness to the Gospel. Congregations that have been served well by our endorsed interim pastors and supported by the protocols, standards, practices, and structure put in place since 1999 have been transformed.

Our legacy of transition from the time of Muhlenberg has been rediscovered. The missional imagination of our synod and denomination has been reborn. In steady and unsung ways, the work of our interim pastors and leadership has begun to change the culture of our judicatory and our faith communities. As Henry Muhlenberg preached and taught, "*Ecclesia Plantada*" is the truth that the church must be planted in our world and in the hearts of the people. A miraculous example of this time of reformation is happening right now. At the time of this writing Augustus Lutheran Church—the very same congregation which Muhlenberg built over 260 years ago—is facing an upcoming transition following the retirement of their beloved pastor. The delivery system for interim ministry is well underway to provide this historic congregation with a trained intentional interim pastor.

Things have come full circle in this corner of God's kingdom. The protocol for placement has been enacted and they have entered into an agreement with their recommended interim pastor. The Reverend Canon Kenneth Ornell, who is an Episcopal priest, former president of the board of the IMN, an IMN faculty member, and a skilled interim pastor, has been led by the Holy Spirit to serve this historic congregation as their interim pastor. The leadership has embraced the transitional process that will assist them in discerning God's mission as they continue to renew and embrace their missional heritage and imagination in the "new world" of the twenty-first century.

What We Have Learned

1. **It takes time and persistence.** The growth of our interim process and network has evolved over a fifteen-year period. It

does not happen overnight and requires forethought, belief, and commitment to the work of intentional interim ministry in your context. It has also taken us some time to overcome the negative stigma caused by the harm done by some serving as interim pastors who were not trained and were not skilled in transitional process. When resistance by congregational leadership is evident and based on one of these stigmas, it is best to have them meet with leadership from congregations well-served by an effective interim pastor and process.

2. Gatekeepers must be convinced. It is my belief that judicatory staff and congregational leadership do not want further harm to come to already fragile congregations trying to serve in this new world and culture. If interim pastors want their respect and support, then it must be earned through accountable and competent practice in their congregations. They must be convinced that intentional interim ministry will make their congregations healthier and their jobs less riddled with problems. If not, the shadow of interim pastors will never darken the doors of their congregations.

3. The head of the judicatory must make the commitment. Putting a structure in place for the building up of an effective interim network and support system needs the commitment of the judicatory head. In our case, the bishop fully supported the decision to implement the normative practice of having a trained intentional interim pastor serve in every viable transitional congregation.

4. Judicatory staff for interim ministry. Interim ministry must be part of the portfolio of one of the judicatory staff with full oversight of the network and process. If it is treated like a second-class citizen, it will always be one. Other synodical staff must have a thorough understanding (and training, if possible) and commitment to the process so as not to undercut or inhibit the delivery of quality interim pastoral services. Make sure that judicatory staff understands that an interim network is not a repository for inept and incompetent settled pastors who cannot find a call elsewhere.

5. Collaborative leadership. On the judicatory level, this is essential for the broadening of the quality and effectiveness of interim service. Beyond judicatory staff, the dean of interim ministry, the transitional ministry development team, and the trained conference deans have been vital to the health and implementation of our interim network and process. The more voices, hearts, and hands involved in the delivery of interim ministry, the more effective the practice. In addition, judicatory staff must be intentional in recruiting and providing extraordinary missional leaders to search and call committees so that the work of the interim process can be brought to fruition. Be courageous in filtering out settled pastors and leaders from your candidate pool who demonstrate a "chaplaincy" or "maintenance" style of ministry. Develop your reputation as a missional judicatory in search of missional leaders. If you build it this way, with authenticity, they will come.

6. Financial support from the judicatory. This is essential to the growth of the interim network. We challenged our judicatory leadership and governing body to "put its money where its mouth is." In other words, if judicatory leadership deems interim ministry to be a high priority, then it should be reflected in the judicatory budget.

7. Collegiality is a core value. No stealth pastors flying under the radar allowed! Regular gatherings and consultations are important for maintaining high-quality interim service. As mentioned before, accountability through a covenant for service and participation in our consultations and small group gatherings provides the necessary support and challenge for the development of interim pastors. Collegiality within our judicatory is a high priority and value. Our interim pastors have gone above and beyond, and the results have been revelatory. Settled pastors who join us periodically at our consultations often remark that this should be expected of all professional leaders in the church. Also encourage your interim pastors to stay connected nationally through your denomination's interim association, participate in the IMN annual conference and continuing education opportunities, and encourage them to become credentialed as a professional transition specialist through the IMN.

8. Provide learning moments for the judicatory. Congregations and their leadership should be exposed to opportunities to learn more about interim ministry in your judicatory through local workshops, pulpit exchanges, and presentations at larger gatherings within your territory. We have had presentations at our annual synod assembly, conference gatherings, and our mission fair.

9. Judicatory geography will challenge your best efforts. This is a challenge, but one that can be overcome. Our synod is very fortunate to be contained geographically so our interim pastors do not have to relocate every time they are reassigned to a new placement. In larger territories it would be best for the judicatory to consider clusters of interims within manageable geographies. In the case where interim pastors within your denomination are less numerous, it would be best to consider cooperative ecumenical networks within those same geographic clusters. This would require a high level of commitment and collaboration with other judicatory offices and staff.

10. Recruitment and replenishment must be intentional. We are actively seeking to make connections with potential and proven interim pastors locally and nationally. Even in cases where an individual is not immediately available, we encourage settled pastors with evident skill and proven interim pastors from outside of our denomination and network who have expressed interest to consider training and endorsement so that they are ready to serve when a situation might present itself. The broader your pool of endorsed interim pastors and your network with other judicatories, the better able you will be to meet the demands for interim service. We are training and plan to deploy lay leaders to serve as the transition minister, teamed with one of our bridge pastors for pastoral care and sacramental administration.

11. Wellness and self-care are essential. In order to sustain long-term service as an interim pastor, wellness and self-care must be a top priority. This can take shape in different ways from one interim pastor to the next, but regular attention to this reality by the interim and the endorsement process will assure ongoing health and availability of interim pastors for service. Currently we are looking at providing financial support for sabbaticals for interim pastors and also a more centralized system for compensating interim pastors rather than the interim pastor serving at the current level of the exiting pastor. This will enable interim pastors to have a consistent level of income from one placement to the next and it will enable congregations of less means to be served by some of our more experienced and skilled interim pastors.

12. Utilize the best demographic lens available. Easy access to quality demographics for mission planning during any interim or settled ministry is essential to the relevance of mission and ministry. Currently as a judicatory we subscribe annually to MissionInsite, which, in our opinion, is the best demographic resource for faith communities and organizations available today. MissionInsite is a totally interactive, Web-based resource and the demographics are available at your fingertips, any time and anywhere you can access the Internet. Once the judicatory subscribes, every professional and lay leader in any of your congregations can register and have cost-free access to the demographics. We also can make the site available to candidates interviewing for settled ministry in our congregational call processes. Check out this powerful resource at www.MissionInsite.com.

13. Share what you have learned and experienced. One of my long-term goals, now shared by our interim leadership—

specifically our current dean of interim ministry—is that we have put together a three-day interim judicatory identity workshop and best practices seminar in which we meet with judicatory leaders and currently practicing interim pastors in any denomination. This is our benevolence goal to the larger church. If you are interested, feel free to contact us. We also regularly coach other judicatories that seek to improve their structure and practice through teleconference and e-mail. We are also are willing to share the materials that we have developed for use in your judicatory. Feel free to contact us through our website at www.MinistryLink.org.

Notes

1. Theodore G. Tappert and John W. Doberstein, eds. and trans., *The Notebook of a Colonial Clergyman* (Minneapolis, MN: Augsburg Fortress Press, 1959, 1998), 149

2. Daniel J. Boorstin, *The Discoverers* (New York: Random House, 1983)., 86

3. David Daubert, "A Renewal Enterprise" (PowerPoint presentation to Southeastern Pennsylvania Synod, 2008).

4. "At-risk" is defined as congregations with an average weekly worship attendance under 70 and an annual budget under $150,000.

5. Interim Ministry Network, 5740 Executive Drive, Suite 220, Baltimore, MD 21228. http://www.IMNedu.org/.

6. Martin Homan, ed., *Fundamentals of Transitional Ministry* (Baltimore, MD: Interim Ministry Network, 2005, revised 2006), 83.

7. Mike Regele, *Robust Church Development: A Vision for Mobilizing Regional Bodies in Support of Missional Congregations* (Church Innovations, 2003, http://www.churchinnovations.org/).

8. *Guidelines for Ordained Ministers Serving in Interim Ministry*, Division for Ministry, approved by the Church Council of the Evangelical Lutheran Church in America, 1990, http://www.ELCA.org/).

9. Homan, *Fundamentals of Transitional Ministry*, 79.

10. Martin Homan, ed., *The Intentional Interim Minister Fieldwork*

Manual (Baltimore, MD: Interim Ministry Network, 2005), 9ff.

11. Mobility papers are the official forms used by rostered pastors, diaconal ministers, deaconesses, and associates in ministry and synods in the Evangelical Lutheran Church in America (ELCA) that contain information about candidates seeking new calls within the official mobility process. Available at http://www.ELCA.org/.

SECTION III

RESOURCES

RESOURCES

Resource 1: Approximately Equating Terminology
A chart, created by Terry Foland, that gives terms used for leadership structures by various denominations.

Resource 2: Ministry Transition Process Overview Chart
A flow chart that illustrates the transition process as it is used in the Episcopal Diocese of Michigan.

Resource 3: Training for Transitional Ministry
A short list of places that provide training in transitional ministry.

Resource 4: Annotated Bibliography
A list of publications that may be helpful in responding to transition.

Resource 5: A Sermon on Transition (John 21:1–14)
A sermon preached by Molly Dale Smith that uses a biblical perspective to examine the five developmental tasks of interim ministry.

Resource 6: Websites
Websites that provide additional information on topics of particular interest during transition and a list of denominational resources.

Resource 1: APPROXIMATELY EQUATING TERMINOLOGY

Denomination	Judicatory	Judicatory Head
BAPTIST	State Convention Association	Executive Director Dir. of Missions
DISCIPLES OF CHRIST (DOC) Christian Church	Region	Regional Minister
EPISCOPAL CHURCH	Diocese	Bishop
EVANGELICAL LUTHERAN CHURCH IN AMERICA (ELCA)	Synod/District	Bishop/District President
UNITED METHODIST CHURCH	Conference/District	Bishop or District Superintendent
MORAVIAN CHURCH IN NORTH AMERICA	District/Province	President
PRESBYTERIAN CHURCH USA (PCUSA)	Presbytery	Executive Presbyter
REFORMED CHURCH OF AMERICA (RCA)	Particular Synod Classis	Synod Executive
UNITED CHURCH OF CHRIST (UCC)	Conference Association	Conference Minister
UNITED CHURCH OF CANADA (UCCN)	Presbytery	Presbytery Secretary
UNITARIAN UNIVERSALIST ASSOCIATION (UUA)	District	District Executive
METROPOLITAN COMMUNITY CHURCHES (MCC)	Region	Regional Elder

Congregation Board	Lay Leader	Ordained Leader	Search Committee
Board of Deacons	Chair	Pastor/Minister	Pastor Search Committee
Board	Chair/ Moderator	Minister/Pastor	Pulpit/Search Committee
Vestry	Senior Warden	Rector	Search Committee
Council	Council/ Congregation President	Pastor	Call Committee
Administrative Council	Chair, Administrative	Pastor/Minister/ Elder	Staff/Parish Relations Committee
Board of Trustees/Board of Elders	Chairperson	Pastor/Minister	Joint Board
Session	Clerk of Session/Elder	Pastor/Minister	Pastor Nominating Committee (PNC)
Consistory	Elder Vice President of Consistory	Pastor	Pastoral Search Committee
Council/ Consistory	President/ Moderator	Pastor/Minister	Search Committee
Board/Council	Chairperson	Minister	Joint Pastoral Relations Committee
Board of Directors or Board of Trustees	Chair	Minister	Search Committee
Board of Directors or Local Administrative Body	Moderator or Vice Moderator of Board of Directors	Pastor/Minister	Pastoral Search Committee

Used by permission of Terry Foland

Resources 2: Episcopal Diocese of Michigan Ministry Transition Process Overview

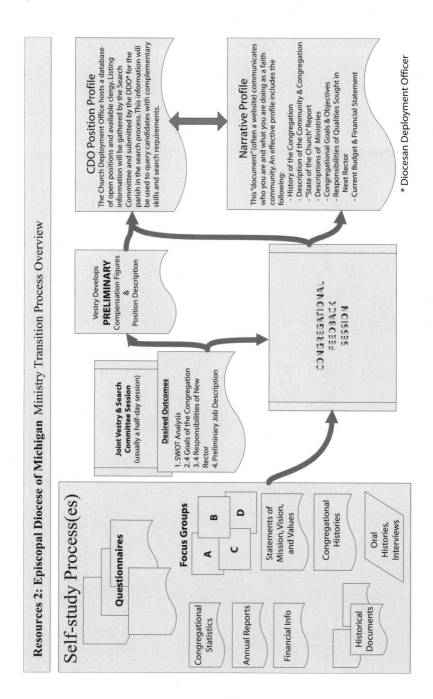

Self-study Process(es)

Questionnaires

Congregational Statistics

Annual Reports

Financial Info

Historical Documents

Focus Groups

A
B
C
D

Statements of Mission, Vision, and Values

Congregational Histories

Oral Histories, Interviews

CONGREGATIONAL FEEDBACK SESSION

Joint Vestry & Search Committee Session
(usually a half-day session)

Desired Outcomes

1. SWOT Analysis
2. 4 Goals of the Congregation
3. 4 Responsibilities of New Rector
4. Preliminary Job Description

Vestry Develops **PRELIMINARY** Compensation Figures & Position Description

CDO Position Profile

The Church Deployment Office hosts a database of open positions and available clergy. Listing information will be gathered by the Search Committee and submitted by the DDO* for the parish in the search process. This information will be used to query candidates with complementary skills and search requirements.

Narrative Profile

This "document" (often a website) communicates who you are and what you are doing as a faith community. An effective profile includes the following:

- History of the Congregation
- Description of the Community & Congregation
- "State of the Church" Report
- Descriptions of Ministries
- Congregational Goals & Objectives
- Responsibilities of Qualities Sought in Next Rector
- Current Budget & Financial Statement

* Diocesan Deployment Officer

Resources 2: Episcopal Diocese of Michigan Ministry Transition Process Overview

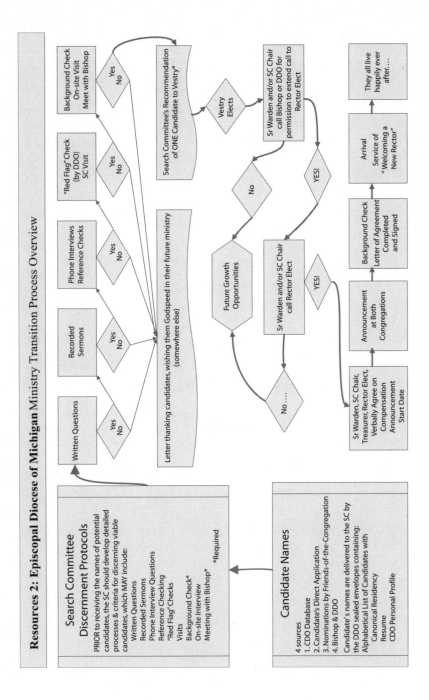

Resource 3: Training for Transitional Ministry

Appreciative Inquiry–Based Leadership Training
Dr. Rob Voyle and the Clergy Leadership Institute provide extensive appreciative inquiry–based continuing education training and coaching for church leaders. Their current programs include individual leadership programs and two year-long certificate programs in Appreciative Interim Ministry (AIM) for intentional transitional ministry and appreciative coaching for those who want to coach from an appreciative perspective. Full program details and training schedules can be found at http://www.clergyleadership.com.

The Center for Congregational Health
The mission of the Center for Congregational Health® is to assist in "Opening doors to hope and wholeness with faith communities, lay leaders and clergy." That mission is met through ongoing training in interim ministry, church consultation, spiritual formation, and emotional intelligence. Other ministry areas include coaching, consulting, and leadership development that are tailored to the needs of the client. For more information about this ministry, visit www
.healthychurch.org, or contact the Center at (336) 716-9722, or write to Medical Center Blvd., Winston-Salem, NC 27157-1098.

Interim Ministry Network
For over twenty-eight years, the Interim Ministry Network has dedicated itself to the health and wellness of church congregations. The wellness of churches is influenced by three kinds of learned leadership skills: prevention of unhealthy practices before they take root, maintenance of congregational health during times of stress or change, and restorative care when it is required. IMN has a skilled and proven faculty with years of ecumenical education experience. It offers regularly scheduled training programs, an annual conference, an advanced skills designation program (PTS and Church Consultants), and membership in a professional association. IMN provides clergy, administrators, and lay leaders with contemporary education and training to help them avoid or reduce the severity of unhealthy practices and to restore spiritual wellness where it has been lost. See http://www.imnedu.org/

Louisville Presbyterian Theological Seminary
This seminary offers a Doctor of Ministry degree in interim ministry. The interim ministry track provides advanced theological study in interim ministry. The program allows for the frequent transitions of interim ministry. Personal leadership skills and understanding ministry contexts are subjected to deepening theological and biblical reflection. The interim pastor has a unique opportunity to integrate theory and practice in special research into ministry in transition times. For more information, see http://www.lpts.edu/Academic_Programs/doctor_ministry.asp

Resource 4:   Annotated Bibliography

After Pastor Ministry

Foland, Terry. "Understanding Conflict and Power." In *Temporary Shepherds*, edited by Roger Nicholson. Herndon, VA: Alban Institute, 1998.
Terry Foland, a Disciples of Christ minister, is a recognized authority on congregational conflict issues. This article briefly covers some of the issues that interim clergy face in congregations where there has been clergy misconduct.

Gaede, Beth Ann, ed. *When a Congregation Is Betrayed*. Herndon, VA: Alban Institute, 2006.
This publication has proven to be very helpful to congregations and interims who follow clergy who have violated personal boundaries with members of their congregation. The authors of the chapters in this book are recognized authorities in dealing with after pastor situations.

Hopkins, Nancy Myer. *The Congregational Response to Clergy Betrayals of Trust*. Collegeville, MN: Liturgical Press, 1998.
This pamphlet contains valuable information for congregations dealing with the aftermath of clergy misconduct. Hopkins also provides direction for influencing the congregation's ability to recover following clergy misconduct.

Hopkins, Nancy Myer and Mark Laaser, eds. *Restoring the Soul of a Church*. Collegeville, MN: Liturgical Press, 1995.
Co-editor Nancy Myer Hopkins has been an authority on aiding interim and settled clergy and congregations through difficult transitions involving clergy misconduct. This book contains many useful suggestions for interims, judicatories, and congregations.

Hudson, Jill M. *Congregational Trauma: Caring, Coping and Learning*. Herndon, VA: Alban Institute, 1998.
This book was written for congregations who have experienced serious trauma such as the death of a pastor or the

destruction of a church building by fire or other catastrophe. Much of the information can be useful to after pastors since they assist congregations in healing after misconduct.

Ruth, Kibbie Simmons, and Karen A. McClintock, with foreword by Speed B. Leas. *Healthy Disclosure: Solving Communication Quandaries in Congregations.* Herndon, VA: Alban Institute, 2007.
Consequences of clergy misconduct can be secret-keeping and rumors regarding the persons involved. The authors give helpful advice to respond to communications issues that arise following clergy misconduct.

Steinke, Peter L. "Twenty Observations about Troubled Congregations." *Alban Weekly,* December 4, 2006. http://www.alban.org/conversation.aspx?id=2848 (accessed February 16, 2009).
Peter Steinke's short article, which appeared in the Alban Institute's e-newsletter, provides help in assessing congregational health by means of analyzing various factors that contribute to trouble and conflict in congregations.

Appreciative Inquiry
Voyle, Rob and Kim Voyle. *Assessing Skills and Discerning Calls (Appreciative Inquiry Edition): A Comprehensive Guide to the Clergy Search Process.* Hillsboro, OR: Clergy Leadership Institute, 2008.
This search manual provides extensive resources to design an intentional transitional ministry and to provide an appreciative foundation for the clergy search process. Resources are also provided on how to conduct an appreciative inquiry summit; establish congregational mission and goals; convert these understandings into search criteria; and move the interviewing process from an adversarial inquisition to a mutual exploration of gifts, strengths, and compatibility.

Voyle, Rob, and Kim Voyle. *Core Elements of the Appreciative*

Way: An Introduction to Appreciative Inquiry for Work and Daily Living. Hillsboro, OR: Clergy Leadership Institute, 2006. This is the Voyles' synthesis of appreciative inquiry, the work of Milton Erickson and his students, and contemplative spirituality. This introduction is provided in an easy-to-read format with sections that can be used for teaching the appreciative way.

Voyle, Rob, and Kim Voyle. *Yes!³ Creating a Purpose-Centered Life in Which You Can Say: Yes! to God, Yes! to your Neighbor, and Yes! to Yourself*. Hillsboro, OR: Clergy Leadership Institute, 2006. *Yes!³* is a small-group study program designed for teaching the appreciative way and growing an appreciative congregational culture by having people use the appreciative way to discern and live their God-given purpose.

Whitney, Diana, and Amanda Trosten-Bloom. *The Power of Appreciative Inquiry: A Practical Guide to Positive Change*. San Francisco: Berrett Koerhler Publishers, 2003. This text provides an introduction to the theory behind appreciative inquiry and is helpful for those who want to understand more about AI.

Change

Block, Peter. *Flawless Consulting*. San Francisco: Jossey-Bass, 2000. When helping an organization make needed changes, the consultant or interim leader helps the organization understand why the change will be helpful. Change is only meaningful when the client owns and is responsible for the change. This is a textbook for helping people discover the pathway to a new future.

Bridges, William. *Managing Transitions: Making the Most of Change*. Reading, MA: Perseus Books, 1991.
This is the basic text about change theory; in other words, "Change 101." Getting the terminology right and under-

standing the dynamics of the interim period are foundational for anyone doing interim work. If you are only going to read one book, choose this one. Bridges' work is foundational to transitional ministry.

Dudley, Carl S., and Nancy T. Ammerman. *Congregations in Transition: A Guide for Analyzing, Assessing, and Adapting in Changing Communities.* San Francisco: Jossey-Bass, 2001.
This guide is a good adjunct to the "four lenses" unit in the "fundamentals of transitional ministry" course offered by the Interim Ministry Network. It has practical advice and easy-to-use charts and exercises for assessing congregational needs. In his introduction to this book, Loren Mead says, "If your congregation is really ready to try its wings, if it has within it life ready to commit itself to the air and to fly, this book is for you. If not, don't mess with this book."

Frost, Michael, and Alan Hirsch. *The Shape of Things to Come: Innovation and Mission for the Twenty-First Century Church.* Peabody, MA: Hendrickson Publishers, 2003.
This highly recommended work gets to the heart of the problem facing so many churches that are stuck in maintenance mode. Their conserving insider approach to things often flies in the face of an articulated theology of mission. Frost and Hirsch believe that the church in mission doesn't wait to reach people or expect people to adapt to the culture of the church. Missional churches feel sent and compelled to reach people.

Holman, Peggy, and Tom Devane. *The Change Handbook: Group Methods for Changing the Future.* San Francisco: Berrett-Koehler Publishers, 1999.
Whether serving as a consultant or an interim pastor, it is helpful to have a toolbox that contains a number of different strategies and approaches. This book ought to be kept near at hand, as it explains various strategies for planning, structuring change workshops and seminars, and process for larger and small groups of people to take steps toward a new future.

Kemp, Bill. *The Church Transition Workbook: Getting Your Church in Gear.* Nashville, TN: Disciples Resources, 2004.
Laid out in short, simple chapters with discussion questions and exercises, this book can be used by groups of any size to help them understand systems theory, change theory, and, more importantly, practical tips on surviving transition and growing in the process. Whether intentional or not, this book is closely related to the developmental tasks as described in IMN training. There are good chapters on congregational size and generational difference as well as help for leaders in congregational change. It also has a chapter on major changes such as closing, merging, and yoking congregations, and another chapter featuring a one-year timeline for using its concepts.

Rendle, Gilbert. *Leading Change in the Congregation.* Bethesda, MD: Alban Institute, 1998.
Using systems theory to understand a congregation is a familiar part of the toolbox for many transitional specialists. Rendle uses this framework to explain ways to help a congregation move from being stuck into a more proactive approach to problem solving. He offers specific advice for being on what he calls "the roller-coaster of change."

Satterlee, Craig A. *When God Speaks Through Change: Preaching in Times of Congregational Transition.* Herndon, VA: Alban Institute, 2005.
A good guide for preaching and worship during transition.

Conflict

Johnson, Barry. *Polarity Management: Identifying and Managing Unsolvable Problems.* Amherst, MA: HRD Press, 1992.
Many of the issues that churches struggle with can never be solved. Beyond simply trying to endure the tension, though, it is possible to find the creative realities that turn what seems to be a problem into an ongoing polarity with much that is to be positive and celebrated. The emphasis isn't on solving

the polarities or making them go away, but on ways to manage them creatively. This is a book from the business world with relevance for church leadership.

Leas, Speed B. *Discover Your Conflict Management Style.* Herndon, VA: Alban Institute, 1997.
More of a pamphlet than a book, this is a quick read and a great tool to use in working with groups of people to help them understand different approaches to conflict.

Congregational Development

Bandy, Thomas. *Facing Reality: A Tool for Congregational Mission Assessment.* Nashville, TN: Abingdon Press, 2001.
This is Thomas Bandy's workbook to go along with *Kicking Habits,* but either can be used alone. It is full of worksheets to explore every aspect of congregational life and help planners understand congregational dynamics and needs. In his introduction, Bandy says, "In the end, only the Gospel matters. Everything else is tactics." This book is a tactical guide to congregational planning.

Bandy, Thomas. *Kicking Habits: Welcome Relief for Addicted Churches.* Nashville, TN: Abingdon Press, 1997.
Kicking Habits describes "a systematic approach to the organic transformation of congregations," says William Easum in the foreword to the book. The book contrasts "The Thriving Church" with "The Declining Church" and gives the practitioner insights and processes for moving the congregation from declining to thriving through easy-to-read text, helpful charts, aand well-thought-out "quizzes." Bandy calls the declining church an "addict" and says that "the church cannot be simply renewed—it must be transformed. . . . Only systemic change will overcome addiction." Would make a good study guide for any congregation during a transitional period.

Keucher, Gerald W. *Remember the Future: Financial Leadership*

and Asset Management for Congregations. New York: Church Publishing, 2006.
Good, specific comments to guide you through the process of reviewing financial procedures—a must during transition.

Mann, Alice. *Can Our Church Live? Redeveloping Congregations in Decline.* Herndon, VA: Alban Institute, 1999.
Mann helps the church discern where it is in its life cycle. This can be a helpful tool in congregational analysis and planning for the future.

Mann, Alice. *The In-Between Church: Navigating Size Transitions in Congregations.* Herndon, VA: Alban Institute, 1998.
One of the specialized tasks of transitional ministry is leading a congregation as it moves through a size change. Using the congregation size analysis originally developed by Arlin Rothage, Mann provides excellent insight into the issues faced during these kinds of transitions.

Snow, Luther K. *The Power of Asset Mapping: How Your Congregation Can Act On Its Gifts.* Herndon, VA: Alban Institute, 2004.
Snow presents a practical plan to help congregations discover how to use their assets to achieve future goals. This could be the final step in a strategic planning process.

Southern, Richard, and Robert Norton. *Cracking Your Congregation's Code: Mapping Your Spiritual DNA to Create Your Future.* San Francisco: Jossey-Bass, 2001.
The authors use a systems approach to understanding congregations and assisting them in planning for growth. They write, "Once a congregation—your congregation—has a clear sense of who it is, why it exists, what it is doing, and where it would like to go, it can then create a strategic map for the future that remains true to that identity even as conditions and needs change." To help congregations do this, they have

identified four systems that "carry, distribute, and circulate the spiritual DNA throughout the living body of the congregation: the welcoming system, the nurturing system, the empowering system, and the serving system." Contains surveys and maps for developing the congregational plan.

Culture

Collins, Jim. *Good to Great*. New York: Harper Collins, 2001.
On the best-seller list for business books since its publication, this book contains many stories and examples of those rare companies that thrive and adapt themselves to the changing marketplace, while many other businesses in the same field sputter along or even fade away. Most of the key concepts explained by Collins apply to congregations that adapt and change.

Gibbs, Eddie, and Ryan Bolger. *Emerging Churches: Creating Christian Community in Postmodern Worlds*. Grand Rapids, MI: Baker Publishing, 2005.
The questions an interim pastor raises might lead people to want to know some different ways of being church in this postmodern world. This book offers sound scholarship regarding the cultural shift that is occurring, as well as many hopeful examples from churches all over the world.

Johnson, Steven. *Emergence: The Connected Lives of Ants, Brains,*

Cities, and Software. New York: Simon and Schuster, 2001.
This book is on the list because it helps an interim to understand the dynamics behind self-organizing systems as they are found in all kinds of places. By implication, it is possible to extrapolate these principles to the realities of congregational life. In the process, the student of self-organizing systems can appreciate the positive and often unheralded aspects of life in the church, while also calling the church to try new things, as adaptive behavior is key to surviving.

Kaufmann, Stuart. *At Home in the Universe: The Search for Laws of Self-Organization and Complexity.* New York: Oxford University Press, 1995.

While somewhat dense and mathematical in places, this book offers many wonderful examples of life-forms emerging at what is a called "the edge of chaos." What many church people say they want in their common life when they yearn for order and stability may be exactly the opposite of what is needed if they are to grow and develop. As Kaufman points out, there must be some balance between structure and surprise. If the system is only "ordered" and it takes away all surprise, it will die.

Sweet, Leonard, ed. *The Church in the Emerging Culture.* Grand Rapids, MI: Zondervan, 2003.

Many of us struggle to understand the implications of living in what is called a "postmodern world." This book uses an innovative approach to tackle some of the subtle aspects of this discussion. There are five major chapters or perspectives, with each author and the editor weighing into the reflective process. While it can be a little disconcerting to find comments being made right in the middle of some paragraphs, this approach allows for commentary that encourages some important dialogue.

The Wall Street Journal

Each day *The Wall Street Journal* offers its readers far more than business news. It describes a world, led by economic forces, which must also grapple with changes in technology, the arts, politics, as well as the shifts in the international political arena. The level of reporting is excellent. The focus is always on the way that decisions in business affect ordinary people in their regular lives.

Wheatley, Margaret. *Turning to One Another: Simple Conversations to Restore Hope to the Future.* San Francisco: Berrett-Koehler Publishers, 2002.

An interim period can be a time to ask some hard questions, and it can be an opportunity to engage all kinds of people in the conversation, even some who may have felt excluded or discounted in the past. Wheatley's work, while not written with the church in mind, nonetheless offers ten questions that might prompt a discussion that would kick-start a church into imagining a new future for itself.

Leadership

Heifetz, Ronald. *Leadership Without Easy Answers*. Cambridge, MA: Belknap Press, 1998.

As might be assumed by the title, the author of this study is aware of the many complexities facing a leader in an organization. Interim pastors will find this resource helpful because the call is to lead a church to consider adapting itself in a time of uncertainty. Having been disoriented by loss of a leader, they have an opportunity to be reoriented toward a new future. The stress felt in such a process isn't something to be avoided, as it can be the stimulus needed to consider change.

Kotter, John P. *Leading Change*. Boston, MA: Harvard Business School Press, 1996.

Kotter's work is so applicable to interim work because he believes that positive change only begins with a sense of urgency. In contrast to some who may want their interim pastor to smooth over all the rough edges, Kotter would suggest that the interim help people identify the core issues and values that need to be addressed. The interim may also be the one to lead a church to experience some short-term wins that can then lay the foundation for the next phase of pastoral leadership.

Spirituality

A Disciples Prayer Book: Gospel Based Discipleship. Office of Native American Ministries, Episcopal Church Center. Available for

download at http://ecusa.anglican.org/6057_4133_ENG_HTM.
htm (accessed February 16, 2009), or order from http://www.
episcopalresources.org.
This offers short Bible studies that can help draw a group
together. It is useful in team-building and helps to establish a
biblical base for the work of the congregation.

Strategic Planning

Oswald, Roy, and Robert E. Friedrich Jr. *Discerning Your Congre
gation's Future: A Strategic and Spiritual Approach.* Herndon, VA: Alban Institute, 1996.
If Friedrich's chapter on strategic planning was helpful, you
will find more insights in this book.

Rendle, Gil, and Alice Mann. *Holy Conversations: Strategic
Planning as a Spiritual Practice for Congregations.* Herndon,
VA: Alban Institute, 2003.
This book is worth buying for the Bible study method alone.
The resource section has many practical applications.

Systems Theory

Friedman, Edwin H. *Generation to Generation: Family Process in
Church and Synagogue.* New York: Guilford Press, 1985.
This is the text for systems theory. Friedman is the "guru"
of this approach.

Parsons, George, and Speed B. Leas. *Understanding Your Congrega
tion as a System.* Herndon, VA: Alban Institute, 1993.

Richardson, Ronald W. *Creating a Healthier Church: Family
Systems Theory, Leadership and Congregational Life.* Minneapolis, MN: Fortress Press, 1996. Good insights that will be
especially helpful to transitional pastors and consultants.

Steinke, Peter L. *Healthy Congregations: A Systems Approach.*
Herndon, VA: Alban Institute, 1996.
Steinke takes Freidman's family systems theory to the next

step. This book and Friedman's *Generation to Generation* will be invaluable to those who are in the early stages of understanding how family systems theory helps to understand congregational life.

Steinke, Peter L. *How Your Church Family Works: Understanding Congregations as Emotional Systems.* Herndon, VA: Alban Institute, 1993.

Transitional Ministry

Geitz, Elizabeth. *Calling Clergy: A Spiritual and Practical Guide through the Search Process.* New York: Church Publishing, 2007.
A valuable step-by-step guide to the search process. Geitz uses her experience as a deployment officer in the Episcopal Diocese of New Jersey to give practical guidance in the search process. This book is a "must" for search committees and deployment officers.

Mead, Loren. *A Change of Pastors.* Herndon, VA: Alban Institute, 2005.
As one of the founders of the Alban Institute and of the Interim Ministry Network, Mead has experience with all kinds of congregations. This book is particularly helpful to clergy who are considering becoming transitional pastors.

Nicholson, Roger S. *Temporary Shepherds: A Congregational Handbook for Interim Ministry.* Herndon, VA: Alban Institute, 1998.
This book serves as a guide to pastor and clergy during the interim time. The Bible studies are excellent.

Oswald, Roy M., James M. Heath, and Ann W. Heath. *Beginning Ministry Together: The Alban Handbook for Clergy Transitions.* Herndon, VA: Alban Institute, 2003.
This is a practical guide to the interim process and is especially helpful for clergy.

United Church of Christ

Bailey, J. Martin, and W. Evan Golder, eds. *UCC @ 50: Our History, Our Future.* Cleveland, OH: United Church Press, 2007.
This was published for the fiftieth anniversary of the formation of the UCC. It is a treasure of information, stories, and reflections on the denomination's history by numerous people. A great tool to use in a variety of settings. Available at http://unitedchurchpress.com/product_detail. taf?site_uid1=20&hallway_uid1=21&search_id=&catalog_uid1=208&link_type_uid1=&person_id=&u_currency_id=190 (accessed February 16, 2009).

Resource 5: A Sermon on Transition (John 21:1–14)

This sermon was preached by the Rev. Dr. Molly Dale Smith on April 25, 2004, at All Saints Episcopal Church in Jacksonville, Florida.

The disciples are back to business as usual. Have they forgotten the incredible news? Jesus has risen from the dead. This news was so unbelievable that they must have had to repeat it many times, yet here they are, back to the nets, fishing once again. And suddenly, inexplicably, there is Jesus in their midst. No special greeting—he simply has words of advice. As usual Jesus turns the ordinary into the extraordinary—it is a feast! Almost as if he had never left. Perhaps the recent events were merely a dream. But they know it is not a dream. Terrified, they do not even dare to ask, "Who are you?"

This Resurrection appearance has caught the disciples off their guard. Their leader has left and they are trying to figure out what to do. How do they move on? Or will they just continue their poor fishing as in the past?

Perhaps it will come as no surprise to you that as I examined this text and other Easter season lessons, I found close links to the work of the interim time. I think that a good case can be made that for the disciples the weeks after Easter were an interim—a time of transition. They had lost their leader and needed to begin a new future. With the death of Jesus on the cross, they felt hopeless and helpless. And then came Easter Day and the prospect of a new beginning. During these weeks that we call the Easter season, Jesus taught the disciples what they would need to do the work that began on Pentecost.

All Saints Church, too, has lost a leader. Your task now is to prepare for the new future that will begin when you call the man or woman who will be the next settled rector of this church. The Interim Ministry Network has learned though experience that there are five tasks for a congregation to work on that are key to being prepared for the future. While the Interim Ministry Network has done some formal studying of the interim time, the process is biblical and follows a pattern similar to what the disciples experienced in the time between Easter and Pentecost. In fact, when we look at what happened to the disciples during the period between Easter and Pentecost, we find them working hard on the five, developmental tasks of interim ministry.

So, what are these tasks?

Task 1. Coming to terms with history.

Luke 24 tells us that the resurrected Jesus opened the minds of the disciples. He reminded them of the things he had taught. He helped them to understand the things that had been said and done in the past. I imagine that Peter would just as soon have forgotten his betrayal, yet this weakness is an important part of the story and Peter's honest acceptance of this part of the story has helped many people, who had their own inadequacies, accept that Jesus loves them. They must understand their past before they can be ready for their future and the coming of the Holy Spirit.

Our present is a product of our past and together past and present will birth the future. Without learning, knowing, sharing, understanding the story of All Saints Church, we cannot get much clarity about the present. This means celebrating the joys and accepting the pains of the past.

Task 2. Renewing denominational linkage.

Jesus reminded the disciples that they were part of a specific tradition: Judaism. He speaks to them about the Law of Moses, the prophets, and the psalms. The present they are experiencing, as extraordinary as it is, embraces their tradition and fulfills it. Jesus continues to talk about fulfilling, not abolishing, the law.

All Saints is not an isolated group of people who come to this lovely setting to worship God. All Saints is connected to Christians all over the world but most especially we, here, are linked to the Episcopal Church. We have a shared pattern of worship. We use the same Book of Common Prayer. This connection opens All Saints to a wealth of resources that will be particularly helpful in the process of calling a new rector. We will be welcoming our new bishop here on May 12 to help us get a better understanding of what it means that we are part of diocese and what it means to have a bishop.

Task 3. Allowing needed leadership changes.

Jesus is no longer the human leader of the small band of twelve. His departure created a void and each of them will become a leader and the movement will grow. Soon others will be added to the leadership team. Matthias will replace Judas as one of the twelve. Paul, who never knew the human Jesus, will become a preeminent leader in the early church. What happens now in these crucial weeks of the Easter season sets the tone for the future. Flexibility now helps the leaders accommodate to the situations they soon encounter.

The most obvious leadership change here at All Saints is that Michael and Travis are no longer here. But other leaders will change too. Soon Tom Stinson will be leaving us. Tom has given devoted service to All Saints—he will be greatly missed. But the resources of the church change, times change, and people have seasons to serve in one way and seasons to serve in another. A vestry task force, chaired by Toastie Hardy and Johnny Gardner, is busy working to restructure our ministry to children and youth. Already plans are in place for a new kind of Vacation Bible School. What other changes will occur? This category also includes organizational structure. Do the programs, the rules and regulations, meet the needs of All Saints? Or is change needed? We will be looking at these and other concerns in the weeks ahead.

Task 4. Discovering a new identity.

The Jesus who appears mysteriously to the disciples is not the man who taught by the Sea of Galilee. He is not he one who sat at a table in an upper room and shared bread and wine. This Jesus appears and disappears mysteriously. He seems like a ghost and yet he ate bread and fish in their presence. This is the Risen Christ, a new being. Accepting and embracing the risen Christ is the key part of their journey toward the future.

What is the identity of All Saints Church? What words best describe the church? I have heard lots of words in my short time here. I wonder which are right. Is this a welcoming family? Or is some other description more appropriate? What is the mission of All Saints now?

Task 5. Commitment to new directions in ministry.

Our gospel text concludes with the disciples in fear and perplexity but that is not the end of the story. In the very next verse, Jesus asks Peter if he loves him. This is a move toward a new direction for the twelve. The new direction unfolds slowly as the disciples slowly, slowly come to an awareness of the meaning of the empty tomb and to trust in the good news of the risen Christ.

These tasks are not sequential; they tend to happen simultaneously. The fifth is the summation and can also be the goal of the other four. When All Saints is fully committed to a new direction in ministry, then the church will be ready to call the new rector. You may be saying to yourselves. Wait a minute—we do not want a new direction, thank you very much. We are very happy with things as they are. Well, that is impossible—the past is the past. I am here only on a short-term basis. Whether you like it or not, there will be a new future and it will not be like the past! The question is, will you help shape that new future? Will you be part of the new future?

The disciples do not have to confront their transition issues on their own. The resurrected Christ is with them for encouragement and support. They do their work and on the Day of Pentecost a new entity comes into being. Through the power of the Holy Spirit, the Christian Church is born.

Like the disciples of the past, modern-day disciples—the people of All Saints—can be encouraged and supported by the risen Christ who will bring to us as to them the Peace of God which passes all understanding. And when the work is done, All Saints Church, powered by the Holy Spirit, will be ready for a new beginning.

Thanks be to God.

Resource 6: Websites

After Pastor
  http://www.advocateweb.org/hope/dplseminars.asp
  http://www.AfterPastor.org
  http://www.aeppp.org/AfterPastor.htm

Congregational Development
  The Alban Institute
  http://www.albaninstitute.org

  Center for Congregational Health
  http://www.healthychurch.org

  Congregational Resource Guide
  http://www.congregationalresources.org

  Interim Ministry Network
  http://www.imnedu.org

Denominational Resources
  American Baptist Churches
  http://www.interimministries-abc.org

  Christian Church Disciples of Christ
  http://www.cciwdisciples.org/Interim%20Ministries/
  Interim%20guide-page%201.htm

  Conservative Congregational Christian Conference
  http://www.ccccusa.com/interim.html

  Cooperative Baptist Fellowship
  http://www.thefellowship.info/About-Us/Who-We-Are/
  Partners/Center-for-Congregational-Health

  Episcopal Church
  http://www.episcopalchurch.org
  National Network of Episcopal Clergy Associations—
  http://www.nneca.org

Evangelical Lutheran Church of America
http://www.elca.org
http://www.elca.org/Growing-In-Faith/Ministry/Interim-Ministry-Association.aspx

The Lutheran Church Missouri Synod
http://www.interimministrylcms.org

Lutheran Interim Pastors
National Association of Lutheran Interim Pastors
(NALIP)—http://www.nalip.net

Metropolitan Community Churches
http://www.mccdc.com/Pastoral_Transition_Process/transition_links.htm

North American Baptist Conference
http://nabconference.org/pages.asp?pageid=883

Presbyterian Church (USA)
http://www.pcusa.org/ministers/interim.htm
Association of Presbyterian—Interim Ministry http://www.apims.org

Specialists
http://imetconsortium.com

Unitarian Universalist Association
http://www.uua.org/leaders/leaderslibrary/interimministry/index.shtml

United Church of Christ
http://www.ucc.org
http://www.aucciim.org
http://www.ucc.org/god-is-still-speaking
http://www.thepilgrimpress.com

United Methodist Church
http://www.gbhem.org/site/c.lsKSL3POLvF/b.3852491

Letters of Agreement

The Episcopal Church, Diocese of New York
http://www.dioceseny.org/User_Files/Deployment/
E-loa-interim.doc

The Episcopal Church, Diocese of Virginia
http://www.thediocese.net/deployment/sample_interim_
rector.html

Evangelical Lutheran Church of America, Illinois Synod
http://www.mcselca.org/call_packet/I.Covenant.Guide
lines.pdf

Evangelical Lutheran Church of America, Southeastern Iowa
Synod
http://www.seiasynod.org/documents/forms_resources/
call_process/CP%20Letter%20of%20Agreement.pdf

National Association of Congregational Christian Churches
http://www.naccc.org/PDF/Clergy/Model%20for%20
an%20INTERIM%20MINISTRY%20COVENANT.doc

Presbyterian Church (USA), Presbytery of Cincinnati
http://www.presbyteryofcincinnati.org/mission/COM/
COMFileCabinet/Interim%20-%20Contract.pdf

United Church of Christ, Iowa Conference
http://www.ucciaconf.org/pdfs/interimcontract.pdf

Personal Experiences of Transitional Ministry

Ben Helmer
http://benjaneourlog.blogspot.com

George Martin
http://web.mac.com/georgemartin1/George_Martin_
Ministry_Site/Introduction.html

Strategic Planning and Profile Development

Calling Clergy by Elizabeth Geitz—http://www.churchpub lishing.org/callingclergy

Congregational Resources—http://www.congregationalre sources.org/

Holy Cow Consulting—http://www.holycowconsulting.com

National Church Consulting—http://www.churchconsult. org/index.html

ABOUT THE CONTRIBUTORS

TERRY FOLAND

The Rev. Terry Foland has served as pastor of Disciples of Christ churches for fifteen years and as middle judicatory staff/executive for twenty-three years. He developed and managed interim ministry programs for two Disciples of Christ regions. He has served as a part-time or full-time Alban Institute consultant for thirty years. Primary areas of consulting were with churches in conflict and/or major transition times. He served on the steering committee funded by the Alban Institute that recommended the organization of the Interim Ministry Network, served on the IMN board for the first twelve years, and helped develop the training program. He is currently doing intentional interim ministry and serves on the IMN board.

ROBERT E. FRIEDRICH, JR.

The Rev. Dr. Robert E. Friedrich, Jr. has pastored Presbyterian and Episcopal churches for thirty years. He co-authored, with Roy Oswald, *Discerning Your Congregation's Future*, which was published in 1996. President of The Ekklesia Institute, he has worked with churches and nonprofits in strategic planning, effective ministry, and human relations. In addition to consulting, he has been ordained since 1973 and has served Presbyterian, Congregational, and Episcopal churches, including nine years as a certified interim minister. In 2006, Friedrich earned the professional transition specialist designation.

LAWRENCE L. HAND

The Rev. Dr. Lawrence L. Hand serves as assistant to the bishop for vocations and leadership in the Southeastern Pennsylvania Synod of the Evangelical Lutheran Church in America. In this role, Larry works with the candidacy process for potential rostered leaders and the mobility process for clergy and lay professionals, coordinates the synod's award-winning interim ministry program, and oversees the work of the committee of deans. He is also the staff contact for the congregations and leaders of the Chester and Lower and Upper Montgomery conferences. A graduate of the Lutheran

Theological Seminary at Philadelphia, Larry has a doctorate in marriage and family systems from Eastern Baptist Theological Seminary. Ordained in 1982, he has served congregations across the Southeastern and Northeastern Pennsylvania synods as both a settled and interim pastor prior to joining the synod staff in 1999.

BEN HELMER

The Rev. Ben Helmer is a priest in the Episcopal Church. He retired from a staff position with rural and small communities at the Episcopal Church Center in 2005. Post-retirement, he and his wife spent 2006 in Louisiana, where he was chaplain to diocesan clergy and caregivers and staff in the first year after Hurricanes Katrina and Rita heavily impacted Louisiana. In June 2007 the Helmers went to Guam for eighteen months for an interim ministry appointment in Micronesia. They returned to their home in west Missouri in early 2009.

JOHN KEYDEL

The Rev. John F. Keydel, Jr. is canon for ministry development and transition ministries in the Episcopal Diocese of Michigan. Since 2000, he has assisted approximately fifty congregations in southeast Michigan as they have navigated the processes of clergy leadership transitions, employing a wide variety of contextually appropriate approaches and resources. John's work draws heavily on his expertise and experience in congregational development, group process, financial administration, and organizational development. John also works with clergy seeking new expressions of their calling and vocation. John is currently a member of the board of directors of the Interim Ministry Network.

GEORGE MARTIN

The Rev. Dr. George Martin has over forty years of experience as an ordained person in the Episcopal Church, serving churches as an associate, rector/vicar, and most recently as an interim rector. He is currently serving in his fifth interim call at St. Mark's in Barrington Hills, Illinois. Previous interim assignments were in Amarillo, Texas; LaCrosse, Wisconsin; Red Wing, Minnesota;

and Poway, California. He is a consultant and seminar leader with an emphasis on church growth and evangelism and an interest in healthy, focused change based on vision and mission. In addition to various articles, Dr. Martin is the author of *Advertising the Local Church: A Handbook for Promotion* (1978; revised 1990, 1998, 2002), *Door-to-door Ministry* (1993), *From Disciple to Apostle: A User Friendly Manual for Church Membership* (1996), and *Right Start: Starting New Congregations*, a training manual used by the Seabury Institute (2000).

LOREN MEAD

The Rev. Dr. Loren B. Mead, a priest of the Episcopal Church, is an educator, consultant, and author whose life work has been to strengthen religious institutions, especially local congregations. He is a pioneer in congregational studies, and brought together the methods of organization development consultation and applied research for working with congregations. He led the Presiding Bishop's "Project Test Pattern" from 1969 to 1974. He was the founding president of the Alban Institute, Inc. He assisted in the founding of the Interim Pastor Network and the Consortium of Endowed Episcopal Congregations. Mead has published four best-selling books on the future of the church: *The Once and Future Church* (1991), *Transforming Congregations for the Future* (1994), *Five Challenges for the Once and Future Church* (1996), and *Financial Meltdown in the Mainline?* (1998). He is also the author of *A Change of Pastors* (2005).

BARRY MILLER

The Rev. Barry Miller, an Episcopal priest, has been an intentional interim minister for over fifteen years. He received a certificate from the Interim Ministry Network in 1991. He is a graduate of the Pennsylvania State University and the General Theological Seminary. Miller also has completed programs at the Church Development Institute, the Center for Congregational Health, and the Clergy Leadership Institute. He served as an organization development practitioner in Fortune 500 corporations while also serving in part-time ministry. Miller served congregations as an intentional interim pastor in the Northeast, on the West Coast, and in the South. He is a member of the faculty of the Interim Ministry Network, a member of the board of directors of National Network of Episcopal Clergy Associations (NNECA), and treasurer of Transitional Ministries in the Episcopal Church (TMEC). Miller is married to the Rev. Nancy Miller. The Millers reside in Connecticut.

NANCY MILLER

The Rev. Nancy Miller, an Episcopal priest, was born and raised in St. Louis, Missouri. After graduating from Smith College, she worked in the insurance industry for sixteen years in Georgia, New York, and Connecticut. Nancy graduated from Virginia Theological Seminary in 1989, and for the first six years of her ordained ministry served as a college chaplain, first at Yale University and then at Trinity College in Hartford, Connecticut. She then served for over four years as the deployment officer in the Diocese of Connecticut. She is currently serving as the interim assistant rector at St. John's Church in West Hartford, Connecticut, which is her twelfth intentional interim position, having also served in Massachusetts, New York, California, Virginia, and Pennsylvania. She is president of the Interim Ministry Network.

INEKE MITCHELL

The Rev. Ineke Mitchell, a native of the Netherlands, serves as regional minister for the North Central Region of the Connecticut Conference of the United Church of Christ. In over twenty-five years since her ordination, she has served in a variety of ministry settings as a local church pastor, hospital chaplain, intentional interim pastor, and judicatory staff. She has been a faculty member of the Interim Ministry Network for the last ten years. She was educated in both the Netherlands and the United States. She received her MA in Christian education from the Presbyterian School of Christian Education and her M Div from Union Theological Seminary in Virginia (now Union-PSCE). She was trained by Peter Steinke as a facilitator for "Healthy Congregations." She and her husband Don reside in Canton, Connecticut.

KEN ORNELL

The Rev. Canon Kenneth L. Ornell has been an priest in the Episcopal Church for over forty years. He has served as settled pastor in Massachusetts, Pennsylvania, and Connecticut. Currently he is serving his fourteenth parish as interim rector. He has also served as president, board member, professional transition specialist, and faculty member of the Interim Ministry Network; vice president of TMEC; and as a search process and parish life consultant. Teaching about transition is an important part of his focus as an IMN faculty member.

MOLLY DALE SMITH

The Rev. Dr. Molly Dale Smith, an Episcopal priest, is a trained intentional pastor and a consultant in transition and congregational development. She is president of Transitional Ministries in the Episcopal Church (TMEC), formerly National Association of Episcopal Interim Ministry Specialists, and president-elect of National Network of Episcopal Clergy Associations (NNECA). She has received the professional transition specialist designation from the Interim Ministry Network and is an IMN faculty member. She is canonically resident in the Diocese of New Jersey and has served churches in the dioceses of West Missouri, Newark, New Jersey, Florida, New York, and Tennessee.

ROB VOYLE

The Rev. Dr. Rob Voyle is an Episcopal priest, psychologist, executive coach, and church consultant. He is the director of the Clergy Leadership Institute and is an international leader in the use of appreciative inquiry in church settings. His parochial ministry included twenty years of intentional interim ministry. Along with his wife, Dr. Kim Voyle, Rob is the author of: *Core Elements of the Appreciative Way: An Introduction to Appreciative Inquiry for Work and Daily Living; Yes!*[3] *Creating a Purpose-Centered Life in Which You Can Say: Yes! to God, Yes! to Your Neighbor, and Yes! to Yourself;* and *Assessing Skills and Discerning Calls (Appreciative Inquiry Edition): A Comprehensive Guide to the Clergy Search Process.*